SEX, MONEY & POWER

SEX
MONEY
&
POWER

An Essay in Christian Social Ethics

PHILIP TURNER

COWLEY

Published in the United States of America by Cowley Publications, 980 Memorial Drive, Cambridge, MA 02138

Cover design by James Madden, SSJE

Library of Congress Cataloging in Publication Data

Turner, Philip, 1935–
    Sex, money & power.

    Bibliography: p.
    1. Christian ethics--Anglican authors.
2. Sexual ethics. 3. Wealth, Ethics of. 4. Authority-
Moral and ethical aspects. I. Title. II. Title:
Sex, money, and power.
BJ1251.T87 1985   241   84-72481
ISBN 0-936384-22-0

for

Philip and Constance

PREFACE

This book is about the basic elements of social life—sex, money, power and language—as well as an attempt to change the focus of Christian social ethics and to recast its basic task. It is fitting that a monastic community is responsible for the writing of these essays. In the fall of 1983 I was asked by the Society of St. John the Evangelist to give a series of lectures on some aspect of Christian ethics. It occurred to me then that the monastic tradition has understood more about the purpose and subject matter of Christian social ethics than is normally recognized. The three vows monastics take are poverty, chastity and obedience, and they frequently undertake a discipline of silence. The vows are related to three of the most basic forms of social exchange: sex, money and power, and the discipline is related to a fourth, the exchange of meaning through language.

Monasticism at its best has always understood that the Christian life involves not only the transformation of our life with God, but also the transformation of all the basic forms of human relationship. The church is called upon to be a community in which these transformed patterns are visible. Monasticism, like all forms of Christian living, is a way of drawing people more deeply into the mystery of God's love, of giving expression to that love through transformed relationships, and of displaying God's love for all to see. It is my belief that the first task of Christian social ethics is to reflect on how the church ought to constitute its common life in order to further these purposes, and this aspect of the monastic tradition is the primary source of my moral vision.

I should like, therefore, to thank the Superior of the Society of St. John the Evangelist and all its members for the help and stimulation they have given me through their generous invitation, hospitality, and support. I should also like to thank the editor of Cowley Press, Cynthia Shattuck, for her patience, encouragement, and hard-headed advice throughout the process of writing. My book, with its emphasis on the constitution of the church, owes a debt to the writings of Stanley Hauerwas. Special thanks are also due to Sharon Lloyd, Tim Sedgwick, Frederick Shriver, Linda Strohmier, Ann and Barry Ulanov, and Elizabeth Zarelli, each of whom read portions of this manuscript and made many valuable suggestions.

Philip Turner
General Theological Seminary

CONTENTS

CONTEXT

I spent the years from 1961 to 1971 in Uganda, East Africa. I arrived nine months before independence and left six months after Idi Amin came to power. Close at hand I saw the first results of a hideous dictatorship and the human cost of war in Zaire, Sudan and Ruanda. From a distance I watched my own country flail about in Southeast Asia as it underwent a social revolution of its own. People often ask what those ten years meant to me and, until recently, I could not answer. I have now only the beginning of a response. For the present, my reply is that I began to see and order life in a different way. Ten years in such circumstances can pry one loose from almost everything that is familiar. For me, at least, "It's as if we had left our house for five minutes to mail a letter, and during that time the living room changed places with the room behind the mirror over the fireplace."[1]

This bit of biography is important because it may help to explain why the premise of this essay in Christian social ethics is somewhat different from most contemporary examples of the genre. For ten years I not only observed the world as a stranger and sojourner in another land, but I also became part of a church which was as different from my brand of Virginia Episcopalianism as one can imagine. As a teacher once said to me, "Philip, where you are from, being an Episcopalian is something that happens in certain families."

His point was that my view of the church was establishmentarian. It was, and to an unavoidable extent it still is. Like most Americans, I am heir to that settlement between church and society we trace back to the Emperor Constantine. In what I shall call a "Constantinian universe" society provides a protective and supportive structure within which the church can peacefully exist, and in return the church nurtures that unity of belief and moral practice that makes for social harmony. In the Constantinian universe we Americans have inherited, the work of Christian social ethics is thought to be the statement and recommendation of social practices that do reflect Christian moral insights, but serve at the same time to shape the morals and politics of an entire society.

As its name suggests, it would be naive to say that the Church of Uganda had no Constantinian ambitions of its own. Nevertheless, this church was new. Its roots were in the soil, but fragile. There was in the air the fervor of recent conversion. More important, the assumption that being a Christian and being Ugandan were one and the same had not taken hold. So the question, "What then shall we do?" was asked first about the common life of the church, and not about the life of society as a whole. No one assumed an easy overlap between being Christian and being Ugandan. To play for the first time on the title of this book, the question of what we will do about sex, money and power was asked first about social relations *within* the church, and only in a secondary and derivative way about the constitution of the nation as a whole.

For reasons I will state later, I have come to believe that the assumptions made about social ethics by members of the Church of Uganda are both closer to those of the New Testament and more appropriate to our own circumstances than are the Contantinian notions to which we are heir. The Constantinian settlement that gave birth to our present conception of Christian social ethics steadily weakens in America. The signs are everywhere. The most glaring is a pervasively negative attitude toward the churches; their diminishing social authority is obvious. One is reminded of Kierkegaard's remarks about his own age: "Our age reminds one vividly of the dissolution of the Greek city-state: everything goes on as usual, and yet there is no longer anyone who believes in it."[2] So it seems to be with the church in relation to society.

It is from such a perception that this book springs. Its premise is that though everything in respect to church and society may go on as usual, no one believes it anymore. It is in these circumstances that Christians ought to begin thinking about social ethics by asking first what moral practices ought to shape the life of the church, not what practices ought to form the common life of society as a whole.

The place to begin is not with the constitution of society, but with the constitution of the church. The first question for Christians is not how Americans or Germans or Chinese ought to order their sexual, economic and political relations, but how these engagements ought to be ordered and lived out among Christians. If we begin this way, rather than in the Constantinian mold, two things will happen. The first is that the common life of Christians will have greater integrity and so serve better to make visible both the nature of God and the character and quality of life he provides in his kingdom. The second is that out of the struggle to form a life which reflects God's desire and will for us, Christians will gain a social and political vision that more fully reflects God's intentions for social life. Along with this vision they will acquire both skill and power as well, to undertake (even from a weak and anonymous position) the transformation of the social order.

The premise is a simple one and just a little reflection on our circumstances will, I believe, prove it convincing. There are three observations about the present state of American society that have become truisms. First, we live in a period of rapid social and technological change; second, the religious and moral beliefs of our society are becoming increasingly diverse; third, our social life is built upon thoroughly secular assumptions. Change, diversity and secularism are by now familiar companions, but we are not yet at ease with them. Everyone's teeth have been set on edge, but America's mainline churches have been particularly disquieted and their membership has been thrown into a state of disarray and confusion. Change, diversity and secularism mean that the churches no longer serve as the moral arbiters of society, nor do they articulate and maintain a moral consensus to undergird our social institutions. It seems that the mainline churches cannot even shape the basic beliefs and practices of their own membership. Significant numbers believe such an attempt should be abandoned altogether and replaced by a simple affirmation of diversity.

For these reasons, it may be more accurate to call our major Christian bodies denominations and not churches. I mean by this suggestion only that a church is a church precisely because it does have some ability to shape the mind and life of its membership. When a church is no longer able to do that, when its membership does not expect or desire its guidance in faith and morals and its clergy believe their pastoral role is to affirm each in their difference, we are left with a voluntary association and not a church. Another name will have to be found for such a grouping, and for the moment denomination will serve as well as any.

The Constantinian premise, then, no longer accords with social reality; broad agreements about faith and morals no longer exist. The "common" life of the churches is less and less common, and they can neither state nor maintain a moral consensus. The denominations themselves are dimly aware of these changed circumstances, but like the emperor before he was told the truth, have not yet seen their own nakedness. As one might expect, however, even a dim awareness that things are not quite as they seem has power to provoke reaction. There have been three that are of particular importance. Taking a lead from Ernst Troeltsch, I shall call them neo-Constantinianism, sectarianism, and mysticism. Each reaction makes some sense. Each has its own strengths. Each, however, contains a distortion that skews the nature of Christian social ethics and so each provides a foil for the views I wish to state and defend.

By neo-Constantinianism, I mean those movements and parties within America's denominations that seek to recapture moral influence both among their own membership and within the structures of society, and by so doing reestablish themselves as churches. Neo-Constantinianism comes in a variety of forms. Both the moral majority and many of those members of the Christian left who march behind one or another of the liberationist banners, hawk, beneath their different packaging, the same product. Both wish to establish themselves once more as the conscience of the nation; both make a direct appeal to Christian foundations. Their theologies and their views about what a Christian conscience demand are quite different, as is their understanding of what a "Christian society" ought to be. Both nevertheless seek a "Christian society" and with it the reestablishment of a Constantinian universe. It may be that the Christian right and the Christian left hate each other because they are like the two feuding brothers, Jacob and Esau, children of the same father locked in a deadly struggle over an inheritance each wants but is unwilling to share. The sad fact is, however, that what both want, neither can have. There seems to be no way to reestablish a Constantinian settlement in a society which is at root secular, and in which liberal ideas about social diversity have taken such deep root.

Sectarians are convinced that such a project is both impossible and wrong. Sectarianism is presently expressed by certain attitudes and groups within the mainline denominations, in experimental communities that continue to spring up, and in the symbolic power still carried by earlier experiments such as the Mennonites and Shakers. The sectarian mind is convinced that society, as such, cannot be redeemed and sanctified. Any attempt to do so ends in the corruption of the lives of believers. To play any variation of the establishmentarian game is to enter a contest that cannot be won.

Sectarians thus view the collapse of Constantinianism with both satisfaction and anticipation. The demise of "civil religion" may convince many of what sectarians have always believed, namely, that the sanctification of life takes place not in "the world," but in a faithful community wherein true belief can be maintained. Sectarians unite both dogma and social ethics within a faithful community, which is to be a light that shines in the darkness, and it is this witness that constitutes the true mission of the church. To identify that mission with something like "the redemption of the social order" is to betray the Christian calling.

The third reaction is what Troeltsch and, more recently, Robert Bellah have called mysticism. Bellah claims his research reveals this reaction to be the most common one among the present membership of what were America's mainline churches.

By mysticism neither Troeltsch nor Bellah nor I mean metaphysical beliefs and spiritual disciplines, but rather an amorphous and highly private set of religious beliefs that elevate matters of individual interest and taste and, at the same time, disparage Christian social ethics as a highly suspect, if not distasteful, enterprise. Bellah notes that mysticism is found most frequently among educated, affluent people, who seek a free spirituality and shun both dogma and moral discipline. Ecclesiastical authority counts for little. They view the church as a voluntary association where they can find help and companionship—others of like spirit and like mind. In their search for meaning, followers of this way selectively combine Christian belief and practice with a potpourri of others gathered from the environing culture. The mystical type is eclectic. It holds to a vague form of progressivism, coupled with a developmental view of human consciousness and human progress.

After a brief survey of these characteristics, Bellah concludes that mysticism "lacks any effective social discipline,"
adding that

> contemporary mysticism is the logical descendant of
> Thomas Paine's "My mind is my church," or Jefferson's
> "I am a sect myself." If pursued with thoroughness it
> would produce over 200 million churches, one for each
> American.[3]

If indeed mysticism is the predominant reaction among
America's denominations, the prospect for Christian social
ethics seems dim. The reestablishment of a Constantinian
universe seems unlikely. It looks also as if the sectarian charge
against Constantinianism is in large measure correct: the
Constantinian project appears always to end with the capture
of the mind and life of the church by the social and political
structure it believes itself called to transform. The character
of the times, on occasion, makes it appear that the sectarian
option is perhaps the only way left. Nevertheless, sectarianism is also fatally flawed. Like Constantinianism, sectarianism offers a social ethic; unlike Constantinian social ethics,
however, sectarian ethics are only for the sect. They do not
touch on the general structures of society. I have already
made it clear that I have considerable sympathy for the sectarian point of view—but only as a starting point. The sectarians save the church from pusillanimous surrender to the
surrounding culture, but in refusing to speak a morally constructive word about the institutions of society, they both
undervalue the world and leave it to its own devices. In
turning away from the world, the sect becomes parasitic on
a society it despises and legalistic and stultifying in its common life. Most seriously, the sectarian seems always to become self-righteous and fails, in a manner that is peculiarly
destructive, to notice that the ways of the world are very
much a part of the life of the elect community.

This application of Troeltsch's sociology of religion to

the reaction of the churches in a post-Constantinian age serves to expose some of the reasons for our difficulty in finding a way ahead for Christian social ethics. The models we have inherited seem inadequate to our circumstances. We need to find a better way to conceive of the foundations, task and subject matter of Christian social ethics—one that avoids the antinomianism and social indifference of mysticism, yet brings into creative and mutually correcting tension the sectarian concern for the constitution of the church and the neo-Constantinian dedication to a free and just social order.

A hint about the way ahead has already appeared. The sectarians are correct in holding that Christian social ethics ought to begin with the common life of the church. Holy Scripture and the history of the church both indicate that Christians are called first to live with one another in a way that both seeks to express and disclose to others the new form of life characteristic of the kingdom of God, and at the same time keeps or guards Christians in that life. In this view, Christian social ethics is an expression of new life in the kingdom of God, connected with both the church's proclamation and the process of sanctification. To avoid this starting point is, I believe, to surrender *ab initio* to the ways of the world and to fall immediately into the cultural captivity characteristic of all forms of Constantinianism.

Nevertheless, Christian belief and experience require that it be only a starting point—that it be supplemented by a positive relation to society. Some link must be made between the common life of the faithful community and the life of the world God both creates and redeems, between a social ethic for the church and one for the society as a whole.

One way particularly in vogue at the moment is to say that the kingdom takes form in and through the structures of society. Thus Christian social ethics becomes an attempt to read the hand of God in social and political life, and then cooperate with this providential leading. The worrying thing about this view is the privileged knowledge its devotees claim to have about God's views, together with the fanati-

cism that seems to accompany anyone who claims such intimate knowledge of God's ways and means. It undervalues the place of the church in God's scheme of things, gives little attention to its formation and inner life, and introduces a dubious link between divine providence and historical progress.

A more adequate statement theologically, and one truer to the facts of life, claims to say that the saving power of God is manifest first in the new life taking form within the common life of the church, and insists that it is this new life which provides a way to order social relations. In struggling to live a life that more nearly accords with life in the kingdom of God, Christians learn more about God and hence more about the structure and law of life itself. As I will try to show, the structure is one of reciprocity and the law is one of love. Knowledge of this structure and law come through participation in the common life of the church, and can give Christians a vision of the sort of common life God intends not merely for the church, but for society as a whole. Life together among Christians can also give them motive, skill and power to enter the general life of society and there seek with all people of good will to bring about a pattern of social relations which more closely approximates the form and quality of life that will be obtained in God's kingdom. T Christians can recommend and work to bring about app imations of their vision which are accessible to all pec without making specific reference to religious belief. can hope to provide *good reasons* that in no visible way upon specifically Christian foundations or require dire of a Christian vocabulary. Because their social vision upon the law of life itself, Christians may hope that the will prove more than patient with the social vision the to recommend.

Those who think they hear in these lines echoes voice of Dietrich Bonhoeffer are correct. He saw first modern world had no desire for "authority"; in my no wish for a Constantinian universe in which the

served as spiritual and moral arbiter for society as a whole. He recognized, in consequence, the necessity for Christians to enter the present age without benefit of religious authority and religious language. He thus suggested that "religionless Christianity" must be the form of life adopted by Christians constrained by love to take part in the ordering and governance of society.

Bonhoeffer saw something else as well, however. The source of the vision, skill and power Christians might bring to social and political tasks lies in "arcane," or "private discipline," in "life together." Bonhoeffer realized that "private discipline" and "religionless Christianity" depended one upon the other. As Eberhard Bethge, Bonhoeffer's friend and biographer put it: "Private discipline without religionless Christianity is the ghetto. Religionless Christianity without private discipline is nothing but the shopping mall." To these mutually implied poles I have added only a necessary presupposition. For the connection to be maintained between private discipline, religionless Christianity and the common task of social life, it must be assumed that the law of life is the same for the constitution of the church as it is for the constitution of society. Otherwise what Christians learn to see about God's intentions for social life cannot be translated for the age in which we live. Without this assumption, in a post-Constantinian age, Christians will remain locked in a ghetto and so be lost to a world that again and again loses touch with the deep structure of its own existence.

In the pages that follow, I hope to show that the direction in which Bonhoeffer pointed shows the way to a view of Christian social ethics that is more adequate for our times than those of either neo-Constantinianism, sectarianism or mysticism. These suggestions will be tested by making some initial explorations of what a Christian social ethic might have to say about the four major forms of human interaction it must address: sex, money, power and language. In each of

these cases, the formation of social relations within the church carries with it or implies a vision of the form these relations ought to approximate in the general life of society. This vision can also be given independent support from reason and experience. Faithful believers need feel no guilt about renouncing the use of their own language when they operate in the public arena. Only if what Christians believe to be normative about social relations in general merits independent support from reason and experience will it be possible for them to make their case and hence their contribution to society in a post-Constantinian age. In short, without private discipline Christians will simply conform to the world around them. On the other hand, without the vision offered by religionless Christianity, they will be unable to work for an approximation of that vision in the life of the societies from which they come and upon which they depend.

At this point there are two notes of caution to be sounded. The first is that I do not mean that social relations in the church ought to be ordered just as they will be in some heavenly state, nor that the pattern of relations we aim at in society as a whole ought to be identical with that pattern we think ought to obtain between Christians. All Christian social ethics manifest a tension between the pattern of relation to obtain when God's kingdom comes in its fullness and those relationships which, because of the continuing and ineradicable presence of pride and self-interest in human life, can only approximate this state of perfection. What divides Christians most on ethical matters is, in fact, how great or how small they believe this division to be. The division, no matter how it is measured, means that no society can order its common life on earth as it will be ordered in heaven. Sectarians from the earliest days of the church to the present have made this mistake. So I am not arguing for the constitution of a heavenly community composed only of sheep, whose common life takes no account of human imperfection, weakness or sin. The attempt to establish such a community is, in fact, an attempt to take heaven by storm, and such efforts always prove both fruitless and cruel. They represent a sort of premature eschatology in which human rather than divine ambitions soon reveal themselves.

My point is to the contrary. Both the common life of the church and the life of society as a whole are rooted in the same deep structure. The law of love defines both the nature of God's inner life and what is right and good for human relations. Nonetheless, for what the poet W.H. Auden happily called "the time being," the full expression of that law can only be approximated. Because we remain both finite and sinful, approximation and not fulfillment is the task we have been given. Yet because of the power bestowed by the love of Christ, the approximation that is possible within the church is closer to life's deep structure and to life's fulfillment than that which is called for in our more distant social relations.

What Christians do about sex, money and power can provide them with insights they might not otherwise have about how these relations could be ordered in a more loving and just way throughout the social order. Despite their differences, the social ethics which apply to the constitution of the church and those which apply to society both reflect the same tension and express the same law. The tension is between what Paul called this age and the next. The law is the law of love. This way of conceiving of Christian social ethics has the advantage, which sectarianism does not, of bringing the constitution of the church into vital relation with the constitution of society. At the same time, unlike neo-Constantinianism, it does not confuse and merge the pattern of the church's life with the order of society in general.

The second note of caution contains both a bass and a treble. Participation in the common life of the church will not automatically produce among Christians a more unified social vision, nor one that is utterly discontinuous from that held by many people of good will. My claim is only that the common life of faith has power to make more immediate the law that both undergirds and serves to create changes in the general pattern of social relationships. The care and transformation of the structures of society is a task Christians share with all people of good will. Because this common task is rooted in the law of life itself, Christians and those whose beliefs differ will often find in each other strange and unexpected allies.

The treble note is that Christians whose vision of society springs from the common life of the church can claim no special knowledge when it comes to the specifics of social policy. To bring a social vision into being and maintain it requires a practical wisdom to which religious belief gives no privileged access. No matter what the origin of one's social or political vision may be, in a secular society it is necessary to provide generally negotiable (and this means in part non-religious) reasons for its acceptance. Life within the community of the faithful gives one no special claim to this social and political wisdom, and those ardent liberal and conservative advocates of a "Christian social policy" forget this lesson at their own and everyone else's expense. To place the engine of religion behind a specific set of social, economic, political or military means is to set loose the forces of fanaticism and intolerance in a way that rightly horrifies.

ETHICS AND SACRIFICE

In the previous chapter I argued that moral debate no longer takes place in a Constantinian universe and, for this reason, that the churches ought to give up their establishmentarian charade and alter their basic idea of the function of social ethics. Social ethics ought to begin with the constitution of the church, not of society, and in wrestling with the moral issues involved in the formation of the church, Christians will gain access to a transformed vision of social life. This way of looking at the task of Christian ethics is suggested by the context in which we now do our ethical reflection, but we must ask whether or not an adequate theological foundation can be found for this point of view. Christian theology can provide such a foundation, but the most illuminating way to begin this particular discussion is one step back from direct theological reflection. If we are to find an adequate foundation for social ethics, we must first ask what they are.

In 1925 the French sociologist, Marcel Mauss, published a deceptively simple monograph entitled *The Gift*. He noted that in all societies gifts are given, received and returned. Gifts, he argued, provide a strategic example of the constitutive element of social life—what he called generalized exchange. Mauss's insight was that society may be understood as a complex system of exchanges which serve to express, establish and maintain both alliance and hierarchy. Alliance and hierarchy are the two basic elements of social order, expressed and maintained both by various forms of exchange and by the moral obligations that these express and serve to engender.

Think for a moment of what happens when gifts are received and given. If the gift is received and some return is made either then or at a later date, a social relation or alliance has been established, advanced or strengthened. If the gift received is larger than any that can be returned, an alliance still comes into being, but it is one between unequal parties. In this case, hierarchy has been established within the alliance.

Gifts are then a way of recognizing friends, making friends, and struggling for dominance. They carry always both possibilities and so it is with all other forms of exchange. Whether the gift recognizes or establishes an alliance between equals or hierarchy within an alliance, gifts or exchanges provide the basic mechanism of social life and are the font of social obligation. Social morality is rooted in a society's mechanisms of exchange. Social obligation is literally a form of indebtedness.

Another French anthropologist, Levi Strauss, has carried Mauss's argument a step further. He proposes that society be understood as a system of communication in which exchanges can be analyzed on three significant levels: the exchange of sexual partners, the exchange of goods and services, and the exchange of language or meaning. Social anthropology then is the study of the various forms these exchanges can take and of the structure that undergirds exchange in all its forms.[4]

Given this model of the nature of social life, how may social ethics be understood? We may view social ethics as an attempt to make proposals about those sorts of obligations our social exchanges ought to recognize or create, and about the purposes these exchanges ought to serve. Social ethics asks what sorts of obligations our sexual, monetary, political and linguistic exchanges ought to recognize or engender, and what purpose these engagements ought or ought not to serve.

Society is best understood as a complex system of exchange and communication that can be analyzed on three strategic levels. At each level the reciprocal movements of giving and receiving weave the very fabric of social life. Giving and receiving are not, as is suggested by many of the moral and social theories that now control the mind of our society, merely voluntary, accidental aspects of human nature. They are not *simply* prudential means of survival or self-advancement. Mauss comments,

> It is something other than utility which makes goods circulate in these multifarious and fairly enlightened societies. Clans, age groups and sexes, in view of the many relationships ensuing from contacts between them, are in a state of perpetual economic effervescence which has little about it that is materialistic; it is much less prosaic than our sale and purchase, hire of services and speculations.[5]

What is this "something other than utility"? For Mauss, it is the nature of society itself that demands "a state of perpetual economic effervescence." Mauss believed with Durkheim that human nature is the product of sociological laws. To open the structure of social relations to view is to dispel the mystery of human nature. There is more truth in this view than many of us care to admit; still, it does seem possible to argue that society is as much the product of human nature as human nature is the product of society.[6] We might say that giving and receiving, what I shall call bestowal and counter-bestowal, are of the nature of Adam and Eve just as they are of the nature of their society. Perhaps the universal phenomenon of gifts points to what we can dare call both a law of our nature and a law of society. In both an individual and communal sense, to be is to give, receive and return; not to be is to refuse such engagements.

Resolute individualists can deny such a conclusion. They can insist that reciprocity is not essential to human nature and human flourishing. Yet Christian anthropology, with its controlling notion of the image of God, must conclude otherwise—a conclusion rooted in belief rather than in the observation of social life.

Through the life, death and resurrection of Christ, Christians believe God has made known not only how he is related to the world, but also who he is. Christ makes manifest not only the nature of God's activity, but also the nature of God's inner life. In the terms of classical theology, in Christ both an economic and ontological Trinity are revealed. In Christ we believe God to be Father, Son, and Holy Spirit, one God, in himself and in relation to the world. Since Christians believe that all people are created in the image of God, the revelation of God's inner life is of first importance if human nature is to be adequately understood. The key to an adequate anthropology lies in what has been made known about divine nature. What Christians believe to have been revealed about God's life is summed up in the doctrine of the Trinity.

What light can this throw on the facts of social life that Mauss and others have so patiently garnered? What can it tell us about the structure and law of our own nature, as well as the foundation of social ethics? Granted, the doctrine of the Trinity is an unexpected vantage point for making observations and drawing conclusions about life's deep structure. It is, however, for Christians, the strategic point from which to undertake such an enterprise.

Think for a moment about what this apparently antique doctrine says about the life of God and about what is normative for human life. In their early arguments with the Arians, St. Athanasius and his supporters were convinced, as the Arians were not, that God as revealed in Christ could no longer be viewed as the Greeks had done—as a unitary, self-contained and absolute being who, in W.H. Auden's words, "has no need of friends and is indifferent to a world of Time and Quantity and Horror which he did not create."[7] In the debates between the Arians and the Orthodox it is clear that the issue was not how the three distinct persons of the Trinity can still be one God. This issue was, rather, whether God was one, undifferentiated and self-contained, as the Arians claimed, or living, dynamic and related both to himself and to a world that is both contingent and sinful. The doctrine of the Trinity proved, once the battle between the Arians and the Orthodox was joined, to be central to the Orthodox defense of their position.

Athanasius, in order to defend the belief that God is a living, related God, insisted that the second person of the Trinity, the Son, is not a *creature,* "made" in some way by God to do what an absolute God by definition cannot do— fashion and govern a finite and sinful world. To dispel this notion, Athanasius insisted that the Son is "eternally begotten" of the Father. In making this claim, Athanasius wished to state something about the inner life of God that was anathema to the Arians. The Son is both dependent on the Father and fully equal to him. The Son is like a child "begotten," but still equal to the Father who begets him. What was Athanasius saying about God's inner and eternal nature? Simply stated, he held that it is of the eternal nature of God to bestow, present, or give himself. The Son is fully God because God the Father eternally bestows or gives to him all that he is, yet dependent because all that he has comes from the Father. Similarly the Father is dependent upon the Son; he refuses to force the return of what he has given.

Unlike Arius, Athanasius thus believed dependency to be a part of the divine life. This dependence, however, is not one of imperfection—it is "begotten" by love, and in love the dependent Son gives back all that he is given to the Father. All that is given is returned. God thus lives and is love. His inner life eternally is one of giving, receiving and returning, and all this takes place in and through the Spirit. Between Father, Son, and Spirit there is coinherence, a total presence, a giving, receiving, and returning.

We may now return to Mauss's analysis of the nature of society and draw a helpful analogy. The doctrine of the Trinity places presence and exchange at the heart of the inner life of God. It is of God's eternal nature to bestow all he is and receive back all he has given. The traditional way of saying this is, "God is love." To use a more psychological and less social metaphor, we might say that God is entirely present to himself and so there is no darkness. Only light. There is nothing differentiated that has not been incorporated.

To return to the social metaphor, all that is given is returned. All that is returned has first been given, and on neither side of the exchange is there an unaccounted-for remainder held back. There is total presence. God lives and is love because presence, bestowal, and counter-bestowal lie eternally at the heart of his life.

If then we believe that God has been revealed as Father, Son, and Holy Spirit, and that we are created in the image of God, how are we to read the sociological text Mauss and Levi Strauss spread before us? We will read it as the tracing of an eternal law of being—the law of reciprocity or love that is God's eternal nature and so the law of all things created in God's image. The Trinity thus proves to be for Christians not only the central element in their doctrine of God, but also to be the foundation of anthropology and of all social ethics. Presence, reciprocity, giving, receiving and returning define the deep structure of both divine and human life. What, however, is the nature or quality of this presence and reciprocity? What, in other words, is the nature of the love that characterizes both God's inner life and the normative pattern of the social life?

Once again, the life, death and resurrection of Christ makes known to the eyes of faith something at which general human experience can only hint. Love defines the character of the pattern of presence and reciprocity that gives life its form. To love is to be fully present to and for another, to bestow oneself *fully and truly*, and in that bestowal to trust that the gift given, oneself, has power to call forth its return. Here we see the true nature of love and we see the nature of its power. Love is presence and gift, pure and simple. It has no need to hide or to force a return. Love as honest presence and gift has power through the Spirit to beget love and elicit love in return. So God bestows himself upon Christ and Christ returns all that is given to God. In like manner Christ gives himself to us, trusting that the presence and gift of his life has through the Spirit power to draw forth its own return.

With this knowledge of the pattern and character of life's deep structure before us, we may read once more the sociological text. Now we can see further into its meaning and its ambiguity. Social life has as its defining form bestowal and counter-bestowal. Seen through the lens of the doctrine of the Trinity, this form appears as a tracing of divine life itself. The pattern appears, however, only as a tracing—what St. Augustine called a "vestige of the Trinity." The form of our life together is merely a tracing because the gifts we give, receive and return are never gifts pure and simple. Our exchanges are not altogether free; in part, they are attempts to hide ourselves, and to bind others to us. In his essay, Mauss noted that the exchanges of social life appear to be fully voluntary. In fact, there is always about them a degree of deception and a hint of force. Social exchange is often not too far from conquest; it is rarely wholly innocent. Hidden beneath the free play of bestowal and counter-bestowal lies both the desire to hide our true self and the calculated attempt to create indebtedness and the demand for repayment. In the real game of life, free gifts are rarely free; they demand return; they are a means of masking ourselves, forcing alliances, and establishing patterns of dominance and subservience within those alliances. To the eyes of faith, Mauss's sociological text displays the gift not only as an expression of the nature of being, but also as a veiled fist present to some extent in all our exchanges—be they of sex, money, power, or language.

Bestowal and counter-bestowal never spring *simply* from the free play of love. Such freedom and trust rarely, if ever, appear without some impurity of motive or intent. Our social exchanges lack innocence and immediacy. They do not carry our presence fully to others; they often hide as much as they reveal. In the act of giving elements of free play and immediacy are never completely absent, but they are always accompanied by self-interested calculation. Social exchange may seek to appear an honest bestowal; it is never just that. Although life's deep reciprocal structure remains intact, the purpose to which we link that structure is no longer simple and it is no longer the original one of communion in love. Everywhere there is the attempt to use life's undergirding pattern as a tool for furthering either public or private self-interest. Thus, the character or nature of social exchange changes from the free play of love in God's inner life to the calculated movements of self-interest upon earth. Here below, what God intended to be a dance has become a chess game.

The movement from sociology to theology and back again seems a long way around to get to our original question about a theological foundation for a social ethic appropriate for our age. However we are now in a position to ask directly how Christians ought to view social life and social ethics, and to see more clearly how the Christian view of ethics is rooted in their understanding of God's life. For once theology enables us to see the difference between what our common life is intended to be and what it is, we have to ask how our social exchanges can be ordered so as more closely to approximate the character and purpose God intends for them. More important, we are forced to ask how the motives and intentions that divert our social exchanges from their intended purpose and distort their intended character can be transformed. To answer the first of these questions is the purpose of this book. To lay the foundation for this answer requires, however, that the second be addressed, if only in passing.

Once again, in Christ, God has made known how the motives and intentions of the human heart are changed. Love, that is, the kind of love that defines God's inner life, is dependent. Divine love bestows itself fully, but renounces force as the means of procuring its desired return. Love begets love through the power of the Spirit rather than through the force of arms.

It is divine love that is fully present in the life, death and resurrection of Jesus. This love is returned to God, yet at the same time given fully to all of us. In Christ's bestowal of himself, we see for the first and only time in history what is promised in all our exchanges, but never fully present—a gift, pure and simple, a total bestowal of self in which nothing is kept back. In Christ we see life lived as "in heaven," or as in the kingdom of God. Christ's love is displayed in his refusal to play the game of exchange by earthly rules and for earthly purposes. In this case, self-bestowal is in no way in the service of self-interest. Christ's life is gift, pure and simple.

God does not seek to change our motives and intentions by entering the game of social exchange and playing it so successfully by earthly rules that he conquers us all. God's way of changing the social game we play is to continue to bestow himself in truth—as he is—and in so doing absorb into himself the negative return—or rejection—of that gift. The absorption of this negative return into the life of Christ and so into the life of God, Christians believe, is love's deepest expression, with the power to draw from us the poison of self-interest and so transform our motives and intentions. Jesus' death on the cross is the complete self-offering of God and the man Jesus, each united to the other. It is this offering that expresses God's dependence, but at the same time proves to be the power of God that draws forth rejection, absorbs it, and converts the negative return of hatred into the positive one of love. It is God's self-bestowal on the cross that makes atonement, drawing off the venom of self-love and transforming it into the love of God and the love of neighbor.

This divine gift is the central mystery of God's relation to the world. The form of exchange present in the cross, with its power to transform hatred into love, is indeed "a great mystery." Perhaps it is best to try to understand this mystery through a story, rather than in propositions, because of the decisive importance a grasp of the mystery of the cross has for Christian social ethics. Cut loose from the exchange that takes place on the cross, Christian ethics become stiff, legalistic and destructive.

The story in question I first heard told by Elie Wiesel at a conference on ethics and evil held in 1981 at Phillips Exeter Academy. The story concerns the Jewish philosopher, Moses Mendelssohn. It is, I believe, a true story.

Mendelssohn was a philosopher who lived at the time of Kant. Though of modest origins, he achieved considerable prominence. His father decided that since his son had done so well, it was right for him to marry. In the manner of that time, Moses' father made the arrangements. It was agreed that Mendelssohn should marry the daughter of one of the Lessings, who was young, beautiful and accomplished.

The arrangement was considered extraordinary not only because of Mendelssohn's humble origins, but also because he was a man noted for his extreme ugliness. The engagement had about it something of the archetype of beauty and the beast. As in the fable, the couple had never met. A party was arranged. Mendelssohn arrived early and immediately began an intense philosophical discussion, which so absorbed him that he didn't notice the arrival of his fiancée. She stepped into the room, took one look at Mendelssohn, and fainted.

She was quickly carried out. Mendelssohn noticed nothing and continued his discourse. When the young woman came to some minutes later, she gazed at her father and said, "No, I won't do it."

By this time Mendelssohn was aware that something was wrong and asked his father if there were some difficulty. His father answered, "What can I say, my son? She says no!"

Young Mendelssohn thought for a moment and answered, "My father, I quite understand, but I ask one favor. I would like permission to see her alone for ten minutes."

His father said it would be difficult, but he managed to arrange a meeting between the two. After a courteous bow, Mendelssohn said, "I want you to know that I understand, but I should like permission to tell you a story. The story concerns my soul before I was born—just when I was on the way with my guardian angel to earth. Even then I was a philosopher and I knew that for each soul there is another one intended.

"I asked my guardian angel if I could look upon the soul of my intended. At first he refused, but even then I was a philosopher, so I asked him to give me one good reason why not.

"He could find no reply, so he reluctantly agreed. I went right away and looked upon the soul of my intended, and do you know what?

"She was the ugliest woman I have ever seen.

"I went back and said to my guardian angel, 'No, I won't do it!'

"He said, 'But you must!'

"I thought for a moment and then said, 'Yes, I'll marry her, but only on one condition.'

" 'What's that?' said my angel.

"I answered, 'My condition is that I take her ugliness.' "

We can understand this story as a hint about the meaning and power of the exchange between God and us that takes place on the cross. We can take it that at the place of the skull God offered himself and so his most beautiful child to our ugliness, and in that exchange our ugliness was taken into the wracked body and so into the heart of God. We can take it that God is not indifferent to our world of "time and quantity and horror"; in this gift of himself, God has taken our horror into the very center of his life. We can even believe that this bestowal of life, and this acceptance of a return of hate for love and death for life, has power to draw from us our own ugliness and so leave us in the end as beautiful as the children of God are meant to be.

The point about God's absorption of the negative return of his gift is of enormous importance; apart from the revelation of love, it lacks power to transform the springs of human action. Unless the deep movements of the heart are changed, the nature of our exchanges will continue as before. We will see shifts on the surface of things, changes in the balance of power, but the quality and purpose of the social game we play will remain as before—skewed grossly from its intended purpose and weighted in favor of self-interest.

The implications of this point for Christian social ethics are of enormous importance. Insofar as the Christian life and the common life of the church are in some way an imitation of Christ, Christian ethics cannot ignore the fact that the attempt to transform our social exchanges so that they are freer, more just and more honest is apt to meet with rejection. In this age, before God's kingdom comes in its fullness it will always be necessary to use some force to protect and enhance liberty and justice. Even the common life of the church will not be without sanctions. Yet it is also the case that if there is not in both church and society some attempt to absorb the negative elements of our exchanges, the deep motives, intentions and purposes of our common life will be given over increasingly to the forces of egotism. Thus Christian social ethics cannot concern itself simply with the quality of our sexual, economic and political relations, nor merely with how aggressive and self-interested exchanges can be checked by the judicious use of power. A Christian social ethic must concern itself also with the transformation of the aggressive and self-interested offerings we seem always inclined to make.

This mandate for Christian social ethics applies to exchanges in the church and in society as a whole. The extent to which self-interest can be transformed by sacrifice is far greater within the body of the church; even so, love's power to absorb its own rejection is never utterly absent, and the general health of society is vitally dependent upon this hint of the atoning power of sacrifice. The possibility for the transformation of social relations through sacrifice, through restraint rather than force, is present in all circumstances, even if only to a minute extent. It is a part of the job of Christian social ethics to point this fact out to believers and non-believers alike. Because the sacrifice of Christ displays the law of life itself, Christians will find that their advocacy of restraint, patience, sacrifice and magnanimity will be shared by and convincing to many who do not share their religious beliefs.

Christian ethics is born out of the tension between life as God intends it to be in his kingdom, and the limits that the continuing presence of self-interest and contingency place upon its full realization. The form and manner of life characterizing God's kingdom is the fulfillment of God's intentions and purposes embedded in the created order itself. Giving, receiving and returning constitute life's deep structure. The perfection of life's structure and law will come when bestowal and counter-bestowal become gifts pure and simple—when they are given for another's benefit and carry fully the presence of the giver. In this state, God's gift of himself to each of his creatures and children will be fully returned to God and fully shared among the recipients of divine life and divine love. Thus, in the kingdom of heaven, "God will be all in all." His life and love will call forth their return, and so all things will be joined in love for God. In this sense, love alone proves to be eternal. Everything else passes away. It is for this state of being we pray when we say, "Thy kingdom come."

Christian ethics is itself a part of the order of things that is passing away. Its work continues only because God is not yet all in all. For the time being ethics must concern itself not only with the transformation of our sexual, economic and political engagements, but also with the transformation of our motives, intentions and purposes. It has an outer focus on the forms of social exchange and an inner focus on the motives, intentions and purposes of the mind and heart. God's bestowal of himself calls for this response as the appropriate form of counter-bestowal, as the expression of love and adoration, as a means of holding fast to a new way of living and showing to others not only who God is, but also what response he seeks to elicit.

Christian social ethics begins with the constitution of the church. Yet anyone who has caught a glimpse of life's structure, law and purpose must concern themselves also with the constitution of society. Since one deep structure, underlies social life in all its forms, believers will be pushed by love to seek in all forms of social life a close approximation of their vision. The transformation of social structure, motive and intention will prove more difficult and less extensive in the life of society than in the common life of the church. Nonetheless, analogous forms of transformation must be sought in both. In these efforts we have considerable reason to hope. There is good reason to think that believers can share goals and purposes with all people of good will in respect to social order itself, even if agreement about political means lies out of reach. The religious sources of their vision will probably be both well known and visible, but they are not negotiable in the marketplace of the modern world where exchanges take place in a secular and diverse coinage. Christians whose vision is shaped by the expectation of another kingdom will have to make their way in a foreign language and by means of a strange currency—language and currency of human reason and experience.

They may have confidence, however, in their ability to make their way. All forms of exchange must approximate life's structure and law or else tend to disintegrate, leading not only toward the collapse of society, but also the eclipse of human nature. Reason and experience will provide Christians with negotiable means of both stating and testing their point of view. They may have confidence that history will not simply go to the winners. In the very nature of things there is a self-correcting structure and a law that cannot be mocked, which align themselves against any who move too arrogantly and too far from the nature we have been given and the destiny to which we are called.

REVISIONIST SEX

This chapter and the next are about sex—a subject that normally interests people. We talk a lot about sex, but we often talk a lot of nonsense. It is amazing that a subject that takes up so much of our attention is so poorly understood and so ridiculously discussed. I hope that I do not add yet more foolishness to the conversation. I can only hope to avoid my own brand of idiocy if I locate the remarks and observations I have to make within an adequate framework. If what I have to say springs from a grasp of the purpose, subject matter, foundations, and context of Christian ethics rather than from random observation, there might be a real chance of saying something useful. Apart from such a perspective, at best I might manage to be interesting. Interesting remarks about sex are hardly what is needed, however.

What we need is a way to grasp the nature of our sexual engagements and a way to order them so that we enhance rather than diminish their meaning and power. What our society lacks is just such a perspective, an adequate metaphor for understanding and ordering our sexual lives. As a result, we talk a lot, but flounder—we are fast losing the ability to understand our most basic form of relationship. It is my strongest conviction that a review of the purpose, subject matter, foundations, and context of Christian social ethics will lead us to rediscover the metaphor we need.

Although this chapter is about the very earthy business of lovemaking, I want to begin with a summary of the rather theoretical discussion just finished to see what its relation is to the particular question of the ethics of sex. How might a grasp of the purpose, subject matter, foundations, and context of Christian social ethics help us grasp more adequately the nature of our sexual engagements? How might such an exercise add to their meaning and power?

The *purpose* of Christian social ethics is, first, to order our common life in such a way that both as a community and as individuals we are led more deeply into the life of God. It is, in the second place, to give expression to God's love for our brothers and sisters in Christ and to display this love so all may see and believe. These purposes may seem rather high goals to set for governing something as primal as sexual relations, but through the ages Christians have, at their best, insisted that the church in its common life ought to aim at nothing less.

The *subject matter* of Christian social ethics is the same as any form of social ethic. It is the ordering of the basic forms of social exchange—sex, money, power, and language. Any community must order these exchanges if it is to continue to exist as a community. Christian social ethics cannot avoid making normative proposals about each of these, a statement that may seem both obvious and unnecessary. The point is not, however, as obvious as it seems. As will become increasingly apparent, there are voices both within the church and in society as a whole that are making an unprecedented demand—that sexual relations as such be singled out from all others and removed from the subject matter of *social* ethics altogether. In contradistinction to other forms of social relations, they claim, this particular one ought to be left entirely to the determination of private conscience. Simply put, it is argued that society ought to stay out of the bedroom—that sex is not a proper subject for social ethics. Sex is a personal and not a social matter, or so says much of our current popular wisdom. Anyone with a grasp, however, of the normal subject matter of social ethics will be aware of the radical and unusual nature of this proposal.

The *foundations* of Christian ethics rest upon the doctrine of the Trinity. According to this ancient statement about the nature of God's life, presence and exchange are the basic characteristics of reality. One might say that together they constitute the law of being. The particular form of presence and exchange to which all creatures are destined is made manifest in the life, death, and resurrection of Jesus. Here all can see displayed the nature of God's love—the character of the presence and exchange that constitutes God's inner life. This particular form of presence and exchange provides a criterion for judging all others. Christian social ethics always represents an attempt to shape the social practices of the church, and to a lesser extent those of society as a whole, so that they express as fully as possible the nature of God's inner life and so the law of all life.

Each attempt to form our social practices on the model of the divine life reflects, however, a tension between the perfect expression of that love in the life of Christ and the possibilities for its expression within the limiting conditions of history. This tension, sometimes called the tension between this age and the age to come, is never resolved; Christian social ethics will always need to be redone. It will be in a constant state of revision, both because Christians have different assessments of how great or how small the tension ought to be, and because time and circumstances are in a perpetual state of flux. "Time makes ancient good uncouth"—so says the hymn, and all of us know the truth of its poetry. This ever-present need to redo our ethical thinking means, where the ethics of sex are concerned, that some form of revisionism is always called for. The question is whether or not the revisionist proposals now being made are adequate—whether they lead more deeply into the life of God, express that love to our neighbors, and display that love for all to see. It is my contention that the major forms of revisionism now being presented within the denominations and within our culture as a whole are not. We cannot stop the clock and reimpose, as the Christian right proposes, the mores and customs of a bygone era; what we need instead is a form of revisionism that makes sex more powerful and meaningful. What we need is not a way back, but a way ahead.

Finally, how does the *context* in which we now do our ethical reflection affect what we are called upon to say and do about our sexual engagements? The context in which Christians in the West now do their moral reflection is one characterized by an increasing gap between the mind and practices of society, and the moral beliefs and practices that until recently have formed the common life of church and society alike. The Constantinian settlement is fast unravelling, and nowhere is its ragged appearance more obvious than in our sexual practices.

It is trite to say so, but we have indeed undergone a sexual revolution, and there is no way that our society will return to the way things were before. In the past twenty years, sexual ethics have undergone a shift analogous to a quantum leap in physics. An increasing number of teenagers are sexually active. Most parents can now expect their children to have a live-in friend before marriage. Divorced and single people increasingly enter some sort of sexual relations, or a series of them. Gay people demand their right to a full sexual life. A host of factors, from effective and cheap means of birth control to changes in our economic system and alterations in our basic beliefs and values have contributed to the revolution. My purpose, however, is not to analyze its causes, nor is it to survey the wide variety of notions we now have about sex. What I want to do instead is to present what I believe to be the most common reaction on the part of the denominations to the vast changes in our sexual morals, to indicate why I think this response is inadequate, and to suggest finally a way ahead—one that focuses first on the common life of the church rather than that of society as a whole.

The best way to begin is with a question. In view of the changing mores of our society, ought the church to alter its traditional teaching that sexual relations are to take place only between a man and a woman who are married one to another? Might such an alteration lead us more deeply into the divine life, give expression to God's love for all people, and display this love for all to see? There are a number of voices saying that such a change is long overdue, and numerous proposals for revision of the church's teaching have been put forward. Beneath the differences, however, a steady line of thought is perceptible. The basic proposal is that the church relegate the morality of specific sexual acts and types of sexual relations to the realm of private conscience, and in so doing teach that, given love and responsibility, a number of types of "non-" marital sexual relations are both good and right.

It may be that within the major denominations a change like the one just sketched has already occurred. Nonetheless questions must be asked. To what extent do these proposals spring from a deepened understanding of sex and a genuinely Christian ethic of sexual relations? To what extent do they represent a turning-away from Christian moral insight, an adaptation to the mind of the times? It is my belief that the new ethic has brought with it both fresh and foul air. Had I more space, I would give considerable time to sniffing the fresh air. My most fundamental conviction, however, is that the denominations want to press ahead without much thought. The pressures for change are enormous because by definition denominations do not wish to ask much of their membership; they exist to meet needs, rather than to make demands. There is enormous pressure for change from clergy in particular, many of whom have already incorporated some form of revisionist ethics into the pastoral care they offer. For fear of appearing judgmental and in the wake of social

pressures for change, the clergy have adapted pastoral care
to cohere with, rather than challenge, the mind of the times.
A number of forms of sexual relations outside marriage are
now said to be morally acceptable, and on the heels of these
modifications in the moral content of pastoral care come
organized attempts to change also the teachings once associated with the churches.

What form of revisionist sexual ethic is apt to appear
most attractive to the membership of America's mainline
denominations? The three most basic types now present in
our society can be handily labeled libertarian, self-actualizationist, and personalist. Each one of them has its advocates within the denominations. Each is a contender for the
mind of their membership.

The libertarian proposal is the most radical. Libertarians
hold that, with the exception of the duty to prevent the birth
of unwanted children, there is no need for ethics to make
any specific proposals about sexual behavior as such. In fact,
for libertarians there is no specific sexual ethic; the moral
restraints governing sexual behavior are the same as those
governing any relationship. People ought not to coerce, in-
jure, or exploit each other, or do harm to themselves. If these
general restraints are adhered to, sexual relations, like all
special relationships, may be entered into for whatever reasons the participants may have.

The libertarian view of all forms of social relationship is
highly atomistic and based upon the model of a contract
struck for private gain. In entering a relationship *of any sort*,
we need ask only what we want, what will give satisfaction,
and whether the participants will be coerced, injured, or
exploited. One spokesman for libertarianism recently stated
their position this way:

> I suppose the society to which they aspire is one in which
> young people . . . will feel *free to choose* [emphasis added]
> the partner or partners with whom they wish to share
> their lives—to choose the person or persons with whom

it *makes most sense* to them to live, in the fashion which *makes most sense*—or, indeed, to live alone, or in community, or to move from one partner to another as life develops.[8]

The second option our society offers is self-actualizationist. Self-actualizationists are close cousins to the libertarians, but with distinct and important differences. Like the libertarians, they lack a distinct social ethic and justify exchanges of all sorts on one basis only—whether or not they contribute to personal growth and wholeness. Self-actualizationists are close to libertarians, but they are more puritanical. Unlike the libertarians, they insist that not just any reason will do as justification for our social exchanges—be they of sex, money, or power—but all these exchanges must be justified by reference to a single criterion. In all cases they ought to contribute to human development. A Christian advocate of the self-actualization position puts the case this way:

Many Christians do see sex as a God-given gift. . . . They believe that sex is good and that sexuality should contribute to personal growth. They also think that the way in which human beings use their God-given sexuality determines whether their actions are constructive or destructive, good or evil, godly or ungodly. . . .[9]

The author then pronounces favorably upon a number of sexual relations that do not meet the criteria of traditional sexual ethics—namely, adultery, bondage, polyandry, and homosexuality. All of these might contribute to personal growth and so should not be judged apart from this context. The same author comments with disfavor, however, on fetishism, bestiality, pornography, sado-masochism, promiscuity, prostitution, incest, and pederasty, all forms of sexual behavior that do not *in general* contribute to human development. No form of sexual behavior, however, is wrong in itself. It is wrong *only* insofar as it impedes growth or injures health.

The previous example has the advantage of a popular style. It allows us to recognize how common these views have become in our society. The following quote from Paul Tillich's *Morality and Beyond* will perhaps make clear not only how common are self-actualizationist views, but also how sophisticated they can be. I dare say that Tillich's philosophical rhetoric stirs something deep in all of us. Listen to his discussion of the "trans-moral conscience." Citing Heidegger, he says:

> "The call of conscience has the character of the demand that man in his finitude actualize his genuine potentialities, and this means an appeal to become guilty." . . . Only self-deception can give a good moral conscience, since it is impossible *not* to act and since every action implies guilt. . . . The good, trans-moral conscience consists in the acceptance of the bad, moral conscience, which is unavoidable whenever decisions are made and acts are performed.[10]

These are stirring words for both heroes and seducers. Whichever course we might follow, however, the action is to be justified on the basis of growth—the actualization of "genuine potentialities."

Self-actualizationist ethics, like libertarian ethics, have the virtue of simplicity: both positions are easy to grasp. Both are in the air and both will play a part in the revisionist debates within the denominations, but neither, I believe, will win the day.

I say this for two reasons. First, both positions can be used to justify certain sorts of sexual relations most people find abhorrent. It is often argued that sado-masochism, pederasty, incest, and pedophilia can be creative forms of relationship, or at a minimum, that they are not necessarily harmful and thus under certain circumstances licit. The second reason is that both start with an extremely atomistic view of social relations, whereby individuals in search of private satisfaction or personal growth contract with others to obtain the goods and services they need to reach their goals. According to both positions, sexual relations—indeed, all social relations—exist for private benefit; they are analogous to private contracts for personal gain. There is little or no notion of common good, only of common interest. Both libertarian and self-actualizationist ethics thus bear close resemblance to *laissez-faire* economics, where the market brings together buyers and sellers for mutual profit.

The highly self-referential character of both these ethical positions in part explains their popularity. Nevertheless, their individualized and atomistic view of social relations combine to make it unlikely that revisionist sexual ethics will take either of these directions within the denominations. Traditional notions of relationship and communality will prove too strong. These positions will influence the debate within the denominations, but will not themselves replace the traditional ethic of the churches.

The third revisionist option our society is presenting to the denominations has, however, a good chance of becoming the going Christian ethic of sex. I would venture to say that among "liberal" clergy, the personalist position has already carried the day. In general, personalists hold that sexual intercourse, though it need not in all cases be limited to married couples, ought always to express and strengthen personal relations, contribute to the well-being of both partners, and be governed by a high degree of mutual respect and care. Thus personalism gives considerable emphasis to the traditional concern that sexual relations both express and strengthen mutual love, and manifest a high degree of fidelity. On the other hand the same argument can be used to justify premarital sex, adultery, and homosexual relations, all of which can exhibit the requisite mutuality, love, care, and fidelity. Personalism combines traditional values with great flexibility about the specific sorts of sexual relations that may rightly be entered into, and this makes it just the sort of argument the denominations are looking for.

It is precisely because of its power to recommend itself to the denominations that this position requires the closest scrutiny. What exactly are the personalists saying? The heart of their case is that all of us are *persons* in our own right. As person we are not defined in the first instance by our gender or by our community, but by our status as individuals who enjoy certain rights and obligations irrespective of gender or community membership. For a person to be a person, he or she must exist in their own right. Personalism is an individualistic philosophy, but persons nonetheless must be viewed always in relation to other persons. By definition, *person* is a relational term, though not one that is rooted in gender differences. It locates each of us in relations to others not by pointing to sexual differences, but by pointing out the rights we have and the duties we as individuals owe whether we are men or women. It is thus axiomatic for personalists that in their mutual relations, *persons* ought always to show respect for one another as *persons*. They do so by honoring the rights of others and by carrying out their duties toward them. In sexual relations, "respect for persons" involves mutual love, care, honesty, and to a point, fidelity.

There are three further points that must be noted; the first has been mentioned briefly, but needs reiteration. Personalists insist that the requisite degree of love, care, trust, openness, and fidelity can be present in multiple and/or temporary sexual relations. James Nelson, a recent and popular Christian advocate of personalist sexual ethics, says in his book *Embodiment* that on the basis of personalist principles, "the physical expression of one's sexuality with another *person* [emphasis added] ought to be appropriate to the level of loving commitment in that relationship." He insists that in using the bodily language of love, we ought not to lie and we ought not to express ourselves inappropriately. The body language of love has a rich vocabulary. The morality of each word we use (embrace, caress, kiss, foreplay, intercourse) depends upon "its appropriateness to the shared level of commitment and the nature of the relation itself."[11] "Appropriateness" is to be determined both by reference to our motives and to the likely consequences of our actions. In assessing both our motives and the results of our actions, we should show love, care, trust, openness, and fidelity.

On this basis, Nelson goes on to say that though marital relations require permanence, they do not necessarily imply exclusivity. He concludes that "certain secondary relationships of some emotional and sensual depth, possibly including genital intercourse" may be compatible with marital fidelity.[12] The crucial example of Nelson's personalist revisionism is his discussion of extramarital—or, as he prefers, "transmarital"—sexual relations. He comes to similar conclusions, however, in his discussion of sexual relations between single men and women and in his treatment of homosexual relations. Each of these may express, effect, and maintain a personal relation that shows the requisite degree of love, care, trust, openness, and fidelity.

> If intercourse is seen in the context of total body sexuality, then different types of intimacy are appropriate for different types of relationships and for different levels of communications . . . Christianly speaking, then, it becomes imperative to ask: given the potentially profound meaning of genital intercourse and the divine intention that it be used for human fulfillment most richly defined, in *this* relationship and context is this a faithful act consonant with God's presence and purposes?[13]

Nelson and other personalists believe strongly that any number of "non-marital" sexual acts may indeed be both faithful and consonant with God's presence and purpose. The obvious question that must be asked is whether the understanding they have of love, care, trust, openness, and

fidelity is indeed consonant with the nature of these virtues
as revealed in Christ. Does Nelson's presentation of these
virtues mirror the quality of God's presence and self-giving,
or does he draw us toward an ersatz world of trimmed and
simulated virtue? It is my belief that love, care, trust, openness, and fidelity as presented here are but pale shadows of
the real thing. The reasons for my making such a harsh
charge will not appear until we can look at the proposals the
personalists are making from another point of view. I propose to do this in the next chapter, but first my second and
third observations about personalism must be made.

Despite the emphasis personalists place upon the unity
of human nature and the importance of the body and body
language, they are nonetheless dualists. They split human
nature between an inner reality they call the *person* and an
outer container or instrument they call the *body*. It is not their
intention to make such a bifurcation, but if one studies their
vocabulary and use of languages carefully, it becomes more
and more obvious that personalism is but another variation
on the body/soul dualism Western society has inherited from
the Greeks. Listen to the way in which Robert Solomon,
another personalist, talks in his article, "Sexual Paradigms."
He says, "Sexuality has an essential bodily dimension, and
this might well be described as the 'incarnation' or 'sub-
mersion' of a person into his body."[14]

It is tempting for a critic to make much out of nothing,
but in this case I think it fair to say that Solomon's use of
language reflects the essential dualism of his view of human
nature. Thus he presents the "person" as "incarnate" or
"submerged" in a body. This body may be male or female;
the gender is not important. The important thing is that it
is a container for the *person* and a tool the *person* uses to
engage other "persons." James Nelson's discussion of "sex,"
"sexuality," "persons," and "bodies" illustrates the same
point. Indeed, Nelson's text may be taken as something of

a paradigm of the personalist position. It well illustrates all the personalist themes and makes apparent the incipient dualism that characterizes the position in general. How so?

He begins by making a distinction between "sex" on the one hand and "sexuality" on the other. "Sex," he says, "is a biologically-based need which is oriented not only toward procreation, but, indeed, toward pleasure and tension release." "Sexuality" is a related but more inclusive notion. It includes biologically based need, but is in addition a "basic dimension of *personhood*" [emphasis added] that permeates all feeling, thought, and action. Sexuality, Nelson goes on to say, can be defined as "our self-understanding and way of being in the world," and as such it includes "our appropriation of attitudes and characteristics which have been culturally defined as masculine and feminine." It involves also "our affectional orientation toward those of the opposite and/ or same sex," as well as "our attitudes about our own bodies and those of others."[15]

After making this distinction between sex and sexuality, Nelson summarizes his view by saying that "sexuality is a sign, a symbol, a means of our call to communication and communion." Sexuality, as Nelson describes it, moves further and further away from the body with its sexual differences. Sexuality becomes more and more an inner reality that characterizes "persons" apart from their gender. Persons have "sexuality," and sexuality is in large measure a psychic or mental quality that is expressed through the body. It does not matter, finally, whether that body is of a male or female sort. In the end, sexuality appears in Nelson's text to leave the physical realm altogether and become a mental construct, a cultural artifact, a product of history, a mode of self-understanding, a sign, a symbol.[16]

Thus, by an ironic twist, in Nelson's book *Embodiment* the body becomes not an inseparable and defining aspect of our being, but a container and instrument that "persons" (who have some inner mental reality called "sexuality") use to say and do things. The person retreats into a transsexual inner world and stands, as it were, behind the body that it uses as a tool. Nelson moves relentlessly toward a person/body rather than a soul/body dualism, stating baldly that what is important for everyone is to be a person who has a sexuality and "affectional orientation" and who strives (by use of the body) to achieve a unity with other persons "beyond gender roles and affectional orientations."[17] Thus the body, by which we are surely first distinguished as male and female, now contributes nothing to sexuality. Male/female distinctions are "merely" biological and so of no final importance to personhood.

It is, of course, this complex of ideas that allows personalist ethics to make place for homosexual relations. Both Nelson and Solomon clearly state that the gender of the parties involved in a sexual act has nothing to do with its morality. What is important is not male/female relations, but relations between *persons*. These are to be justified on the basis of the aims and results of the relation in question.

The personalist argument is a very attractive one in a morally diverse society like our own. If adopted by the denominations, it would eliminate one very difficult issue (homosexuality) and make room at the same time for a number of different sorts of sexual relations. Personalism makes it easier for the Christian way of life (in respect to sex, at least) to cohere with the mores of a "pluralistic society." If the bait is taken, however, the churches will have to do so by covertly espousing this person/body dualism, hence going against one of the dominant themes of Christian anthropology. They will have to stop insisting that human nature is to be understood as a psychosomatic unity—that we are to think of ourselves as bodies with life in them, as creatures and sinners who will die and be raised again as glorified bodies rather than as disembodied, de-gendered "persons."

The final remark I have to make about personalism is that its proponents believe sexual relations ought to be understood as a form of conversation. Once again, Robert Solomon provides a nice summary:

> Sexual activity consists in speaking what we might call "body language." It has its own grammar, delineated by the body, and its phonetics of touch and movement. Its unit of meaningfulness, the bodily equivalent of a sentence, is the gesture. . . .[18]

For personalists, sexual relations are like having a talk, a way for individual persons to get together for intimate conversation. The moral quality of this talking is finally judged by the sort of conversation one is having. Thus, according to Solomon, masturbation is like talking to oneself. Sadism is not so much a breakdown in communication as an excessive expression of domination. In like manner, masochism is an excessive expression of victimization, shame, or inferiority. Finally, Solomon notes that fetishism is like talking to someone else's shoes, and that bestiality is "like discussing Spinoza with a moderately intelligent sheep."[19]

Solomon's treatment of our sexual "talk" has a humor and irony about it that is often delightful. Nelson is rather more solemn in his treatment, but like Solomon he insists upon understanding sexual relations as a form of conversation. The personalist metaphor for understanding our sexual engagements is less individualistic and economic than those employed by libertarians and self-actualizationists. Personalist metaphors are relational even if they do begin with individual isolated persons trying to get "in touch." Perhaps it is the predominance of relational metaphors that covers the incipient atomism of the position, and so in part gives personalism its power to attract adherents from among the denominations. The communal and relational overtones of personalist images sound closer to traditional Christian values and perceptions than do the more economic and self-referential ones with which they contend.

The question is, how adequate is it to understand making love as having a sort of talk? Does the major personalist metaphor really enhance the meaning and power of our sexual engagements, or does it diminish both? I believe that we diminish rather than enhance our sexual engagements by use of the heady and somewhat abstract metaphor of conversation, but my point will become apparent only if we can find another perspective from which to look upon these engagements. This other point of view will reveal the slenderness of the virtues personalists espouse, and the destructive character of the dualism with which their position is riddled. I hope that another point of view will show us a way ahead—not one that is a mindless call to reimpose without justification the sexual mores of a bygone era, nor a senseless revisionism designed not to convey Christian perception and shape Christian practice, but to attract customers in the huge shopping mall Western society has become.

REAL SEX

My aim in this chapter is not simply to expose the weaknesses of the personalist position. It is to offer a better way to think about making love. I undertake this project with some fear and trembling because, as will by now be obvious, personalism is an enormously attractive position. In a morally diverse society, it seems to offer everyone a way ahead. At some level all of us are dualists, and nearly everyone sees the attraction of a position that allows us to speak both of responsible love and of great flexibility in sexual relations. Personalism speaks to deep movements in our culture. It holds to generally accepted social values and yet blesses diversity of "life style" by allowing the determination of what love and responsibility demand to remain a matter for private judgment only. Personalism is an attractive and tempting option for America's mainline denominations as they attempt to adapt to the times and appear once more as the guardians and arbiters of the morals of an entire society.

But if the beguiling wink of popular appeal is ignored, how well will personalism stand up under the careful scrutiny of a people who dare to believe that they have both the mind and spirit of Christ? Only a return to the original sources

of the Christian message will yield an answer to this question. My contention is that these sources espouse a point of
view that reveals personalism's inadequacy and points to a
better way ahead. The investigation that follows cannot hope
to be complete. There are, nonetheless, two sections of the
Bible, Genesis 1–3 and Ephesians 5:21–33, that have been
particularly influential in forming the church's moral notions
about sex. A fresh look at them will, I believe, indicate the
sort of conclusions the church will eventually be constrained
to reach.

Scholars now generally hold that Genesis 1:1–2:3 and
Genesis 2:4–3:24 come from different authors and different
periods. Genesis 1:1–2:3 reached its final form at the hand
of an editor known as the Priestly writer. Who this editor
was we don't know, but we can tell something about his
interests and his character from the work he left. He was
almost certainly from priestly circles, and like most priests,
he had an enormous concern for order. Therefore the account
of creation he offers is designed to show how God brought
order out of chaos and how God intends that order to be
maintained.

The priestly narrative runs like this: God brings all things
(the heavens and the earth) into being, but their initial state
is chaotic. God begins immediately, however, to create a
cosmos. Light and dark, day and night, are distinguished,
and each is given its own time. The heavens are separated
from the earth and the waters are contained so that earth
and sky appear. Within this basic order, life begins—first
plants, and then various sorts of animals. Each is given its
own specie and its own place—earth, air, water.

There is no need to rehearse further the Priestly account
of the world's first ordering. Its basic outline is well-known.
What is important for our purposes is the account of the
creation of *adam*. *Adam* is all human beings, male and female,
and, as male and female, *adam* is given dominion over the
earth. It is *adam* who is to rule and so further and maintain
the order of the earth in God's name. In this way the earth

will become even more fruitful and God's blessing will produce its intended bounty.

This orderly rule is closely connected with the "image"-like character *adam* is said to have. The word "image" as used here has, among others, a political meaning. It suggests the statue set up by a victorious king to show his authority over a conquered people.[20] Use of the word "image" to describe male and females suggests that *adam*, as male and female, is a sign of God's authority over the order of the world and, in God's name or under his authority, is to rule and to order the earth which is God's possession. For this reason, male and female are blessed so that they may have offspring—so that the earth will be filled and God's rule and order extended throughout. Thus *adam*, as God's viceroy, is to fill or "occupy" the earth, and order it.

This excursion into biblical interpretation may seem far indeed from the personalist arguments about sex which are now so prominent in Christian circles, but it nevertheless suggests another point of view which more closely accords with the sources of Christian belief. In obvious ways, the views of the Priestly writer run contrary to the most basic tenets of personalism. The personalist point of view is rooted in the notion that "human beings" are to be pictured or understood first as autonomous, individual "persons" whose sex is accidental to their nature and whose social relations are displayed as an individually based set of "rights" and "duties" which protect and promote private benefit. The Priestly writer displays human nature from a wholly different perspective. He insists, first of all, that being male and female is not something we seek to transcend on our way to becoming individual "persons." The distinction between male and females is written into the order of the cosmos and is good. As Karl Barth said of this passage some years ago, "Man [*adam*] never exists as such, but always as the human male or the human female."[21]

Even more basic to the other point of view I am trying to describe and defend is the Priestly writer's insistence that we do not become a social whole simply through the sovereign choices of individuals seeking private benefit. We are created a social whole *(adam)* and our maleness and femaleness are to be understood first in relation to this social whole—not in relation to ourselves as individual "persons." In the eyes of the Priestly writer, before God we are first *adam* and then within that singular whole we are distinguished as male and female. From this point of view, we must consider ourselves first as one, as a whole, as *adam*, if we are to understand ourselves properly as many, as male and female, and as individuals. We are both one and many, both *adam* and, within that whole, individual people who are male or female. Our unity before God as *adam* has a certain priority. God is related to us first as *adam* and only within that context as individual persons who are either male or female. A recent interpreter of this passage has said that the word *adam*

> enables scripture to say that God created "man" before he created any of man's component particulars, that any person's essential identity lies in being "man" before being anything else—even before being "a person" ("in my own right," as contemporary thought so wrongheadedly adds).[22]

To understand ourselves even better, we might think once more of the nature of God, in the image of whom *adam*, as male and female, is created. God, Father, Son, and Holy Spirit, is indeed one. That is the first thing to say. Having said, however, that God is one, it is necessary to say that God is one in three. Not through logic, but in the life of God, the ancient problem of the one and the many is resolved, and so also is it in the created life of *adam*, male and female. *Adam* is first a social whole, and within that whole we find our individual identities as man and woman.

It is precisely this vision of human nature that contemporary thought, of which personalism is a prime example, find so abhorrent. We, the children of the Enlightenment, seem to find our primary identity not in *adam*, male and female, but in the human individual or "person." The person exists more and more as an atomistic individual whose gender is swallowed up in the transsexual world of "personhood." As the critic I mentioned above notes, it is this great reversal of the order of things that throws modern theology "clear outside its biblical parameters."[23] It is this reversal also that allows us to link sexual relations so closely with individual needs, desires, and life plans, and so to divorce them more and more from their more traditional place as part of a social whole wherein a man and a woman gave themselves one to another within a context that contained a meaning for both and gave meaning to each.

Another source for the point of view for which we search is Genesis 2 and 3. The Priestly author of Genesis 1 focuses attention upon the place of *adam*, male and female, in God's ordering of creation. The Yahwist, the author or editor of Genesis 2–3, focuses his attention on the nature of the relationship between *the man* and *the woman* who once again are seen first as *adam*, a social whole. The Yahwist's account of human origins portrays both God's original intention for the relationship of men and women [Gen. 2:4a–24] and the effects of disobedience to God upon that relationship [Gen. 3]. If the Priestly writer is inclined to straighten things up, the Yahwist has a proclivity to sniff out the nature and content of relationships. So the Yahwist portrays the man and the woman as paradigmatic expressions of human nature and human society.

Let us begin with the Yahwist's positive account of the primal social relationship—that between *the man* and *the woman*. We must assume that the fundamental question of all mythology once again lies behind this account of human origins: namely, how one becomes many and how the many can find any sort of unity. This question is not only the fundamental one of theology and metaphysics; it is also the basic question for social theory and social ethics. For society to be society (be it by analogy within the life of God or within the common life of *adam*), the one whole that is society must be or contain many, and yet the many must in some way be one. If we make normative proposals about the ethics of sex, money, power, or the use of language, we are making proposals about how the one ought to be many and how the many ought to be one. This way of speaking is but another way into the moral issues connected with social exchange, and hence into the subject matter of social ethics.

Does the Yahwist have a different perspective on the relation between men and women than the advocates of personalism? I think he does. And I think once again that this other point of view makes clear the atomistic and overly self-referential character of personalism's basic fault. The key to the Yahwist's view of God's intentions is his statement that the two, the man and the woman, become "one flesh." This statement or confession is, in fact, a confession of belief about how things between *the man* and *the woman* "ought" to be.

Though the Yahwist depicts the original order of the world in a different way from the Priestly writer, and though he is perhaps more concerned with the nuances of social relations than with mapping the order of things, he is still concerned with the order of the world and the place of *adam* in that order. Thus the Yahwist, before discussing the relation that ought to obtain between the man and the woman, insists that they are to "till and keep" the ordered world God provides as a living space. Once again, both the man and the woman are responsible for the earth, and they may jointly enjoy the bounty their common labor brings forth.

The matter of key importance for the Yahwist is that, in this common labor, the man without the woman is alone and without a suitable helper. The animals are not fit. There must be for the man a society whose inner relations are unlike those between the man and the animals. In the society of *adam*, the many are, at the deepest level, one; they are "bone of bone and flesh of flesh," yet they are different in that they are man and woman. The Yahwist thus pictures God both as differentiating *the man* and *the woman* and as creating a society between them. The particular form of society pictured is the one that exists between husband and wife. This society is paradigmatic of all society. In sociological terms God is the "wife giver," who creates social relations between individuals and groups and initiates the marital bond by leading the woman to the man. We may say that for the Yahwist, the man and the woman (as well as the societies of the earth) are *by nature* one, yet distinct and different, and that by culture or social convention (which is itself initiated by God), they are distinct and different, yet become one by the man "cleaving" to the woman and becoming "one flesh" with her in an act that unites both nature and culture.

To understand what the Yahwist thought the sexual relation ought to be, we must understand what he thought it meant for *the man* and *the woman* to come together in this sort of union. By nature "bone of bone and flesh of flesh," they are, in a sense, already one, though they are so in the distinctiveness of their respective natures. Yet the Yahwist does not say that they *are* "one flesh," but rather they become so. This "becoming" clearly carries first of all not a natural but a social, familial reference. The man "leaves his father and cleaves to his wife." A primal society is formed. Although the woman is taken from the man, it is, strangely enough, the man who leaves home and cleaves to the woman. The relation of the man to the woman in "one flesh" is thus closer than any other—even the bond with one's parents.

To become one flesh also implies a sexual relation. Sexual intercourse distinguishes this bond from all others and defines its peculiar closeness.

The most important thing said of the bond between *the man* and *the woman*, however, is that it is one in which both are naked yet not ashamed. In a union of "one flesh," two distinct and different beings who nonetheless share a common nature are fully present one to another and give themselves fully to one another—most of all, but not exclusively, in the sexual relation. There is in no aspect of their relation any shame or parsimony; nothing is hidden and nothing is held back. We must assume the absence of shame to mean that all is presented, that all is given, that all is received and that all is returned. As in the life of God, all is open, all is light. There is no shadow or turning. To be "one flesh" is to enjoy a unity in diversity, and from within this union of two in one to know what a gift pure and simple is.

In the words of Karl Barth, the man and the woman are given by God in creation a great "permission." They may become "one flesh." This presence and self-giving of one to the other is the promise of their created nature, and it is the norm by which sexual relations are to be judged. We can already see that the norms of personalism, with their self-referential, individualistic bias, are but a pale reflection of God's original intentions and permission. They do not begin to do justice to the rich meaning of the metaphor "one flesh." It is to the exploration of this metaphor that the Bible invites us if we are adequately to grasp the promise of our sexual relations. First, however, we must first look away from these biblical pictures of what *may be* and stare with unblinking eyes at its picture of what *is*.

In the second chapter of Genesis, the Yahwist depicts what God intends and promises for the relationship between husband and wife. This picture seems always to raise in our minds a haunting yet elusive possibility. In sexual relations we do long—even if we are only dimly aware of it—"to become one" with the man or the woman we love. Our desire is to be fully and immediately present one to another, to find a unity in the midst of our diversity. What we know, however, is that lovers are rarely, if ever, present in the way just described. Much is held back, much is hidden. And we ought not to confuse this holding back with simple modesty. Modesty is that slight hesitation everyone feels before standing naked, before being searched out and discovered.

What leads us to hold back is not modesty; it is shame. What we are *must* be hidden. What we have to give must be kept guarded. We cannot bear to present ourselves to others simply as we are. We do not dare simply to give. So we learn to cloak our shame and withhold ourselves. Soon we begin to hide even from ourselves. If you will, the fig leaf of deception we place between ourselves and others soon covers over the character of our own inner life. Out of shame we become strangers not only to others, but to ourselves. We lose the ability to be one with ourselves or with others. Unity, purity, and singleness of heart disappear from our lives.

In our exchanges, be they sexual or otherwise, we are in some way always absent to others, to God and to our-selves. Always something remains hidden in the shadows. To be fully and simply present is a state that lures yet eludes us. Our sexual relations, like all our relations, carry a promise that is rarely fulfilled. Something is missing—some absence that leave us still looking, still waiting, still hoping to be *two* who nonetheless become *one*.

It is this state that the Yahwist depicts in Genesis 3. In the process of distancing themselves from God, the man and the woman distance themselves also from one another. They know that they are naked and so "cover" themselves. Their presence to God and one another becomes at best partial; the full promise of their most basic relationship is habitually delayed. It is not good for the man and the woman to be alone, but now we may say that in some ways they always are.

There is, furthermore, within the partial unity that now exists between them an element of struggle. Mutual presence and mutual aid are both diminished. The society of the man and the woman is no longer one of simple alliance, of mutual care and support; instead, each begins to blame the other for what has gone wrong. So the man blames the woman, and the woman blames the serpent—the chthonic forces of nature and fate. A terrible dishonesty has lodged itself at the heart of their society. The man now "rules over the woman," and "the desire of the woman is for her husband." The man has lost his helper and in her place "gained" only a subject. There is a seldom-noticed but nonetheless cruel irony in the man's particular punishment. Not only does his labor now yield sweat, thorns and thistles instead of bounty; he also labors alone. His helper, having become a subject, is lost to him.

And what of the woman? The very "desire" she has for her husband threatens her own life and integrity. She is caught between the pain of childbirth and her ironic yearning for the husband who now rules over her and whose sexual energy may threaten her very life.

This passage is no doubt written from an androcentric perspective. Had a woman written it, the story would certainly be told somewhat differently. Yet, even from the partial perspective from which this myth of origins is set forth, an enormous amount is suggested about how we might view our sexual relations. If they hold the promise of union through presence and self-giving, they also remind us of a terrible absence, a dreadful lie, and, all too often, a struggle for dominance that seems always ready to intrude itself. Absence, untruth, dominance, and subservience provide not a model of how the two ought to be one, but a hideous caricature of the promised bond of "one flesh."

The passage is rich with meaning, and if we let our imagination roam a bit, we may even come to see our own circumstances more clearly. For one thing, in our more egalitarian and psychological age, the passage may suggest to us the possibility of an ironic reversal. Having exchanged his helper for a subject, the man may seek to please the woman so as once more to win her as a helper. He may do so by becoming subservient to her, and out of resentment born of the conflict between her pain and her desire, the woman may be tempted to seek to bring about just such a reversal in the hierarchy of dominance and subservience.

These last speculations go far beyond the text itself. Even without them, however, a rather clear statement about the relation between the sexes emerges from the Yahwist's account. The relation between *the man* and *the woman* carries an enormous promise—a promise that draws us to one another. Yet the fulfillment of that promise seems forever delayed. We know only a partial unity, and this unity itself is marred by the never-ending "battle of the sexes." That battle is characterized by absence, deception, blameshifting, struggle, and futility. If either wins, both will certainly lose what they most desire—a union in which two become "one flesh."

Personalism can be adequately tested only after searching out an alternative point of view with which to compare it. From the pages of the Bible another point of view begins to emerge. But how does it appear in comparison with the basic tenets of personalism?

There are a certain number of similarities. Both stress the reciprocal character of social relations, and both lay considerable stress on the importance of mutual love, responsibility, care, trust, and openness in sexual relations. However a number of startling differences lie just below the surface, which set off a chain of critical questions about the adequacy of personalism. The first difference has already been pointed out in personalism's dualistic view of human nature. This dualistic motif appears in stark contrast to the unitary view of human nature present with special clarity in the Yahwist's account of creation. *Adam*, who becomes man and woman, is, as man and woman, said to be a *nephesh*, or "living being." The Yahwist thinks of *adam*, and of each man and woman, as a body full of life rather than as a mind, soul, self, or individual that inhabits and uses a body.

It would be easy to take these remarks as quibbles, did we not see that the partial and somewhat mental descriptions of human nature personalists favor lead to some rather inadequate and, on occasion, ludicrous conclusions about sexual relations. I shall provide here only the primary example of the sort of conclusions I have in mind, one that illustrates well, I think, a second area of difference. While personalism views sexual relations as a mutually beneficial conversation between two independent interlocuters, the biblical point of view sees in sexual relations the promise of a genuine union between two who are first a social whole, who are made for each other, who are distinct and different, and who through presence and self-giving become in a real sense one. The example I have in mind is generated by the very inner and mentalist categories personalists use to describe human agency. It is, I think, because "personhood" is such an inner and mental way of describing ourselves that personalists like Nelson understand sexual relations as a form of talking. Sex, like speech, is a way the "person" inside our body makes contact with the "person" inside another body. Making love is, to personalists, something like having a conversation. In this instance, the lovers use organs in addition to the tongue to express themselves.

There is indeed a language of love, and it is certainly the case that we do in the course of making love exchange communications. But is it adequate to describe what we do when we make love as simply another form of symbolic communication? Is lovemaking to be understood simply as two autonomous, individual "persons" using their bodies to talk?

If we think of sexual relations as exchanges in which two bodies filled with life become "one flesh," we are apt to have a much less verbal and, I believe, more complete image of what goes on when the man and the woman "cleave" one to another. They no doubt say things in a different way, but they surely do more than have a talk. Is it not truer to the facts to say that they present and give themselves one to another, and that this presentation carries with it not all that they are, but some aspect of everything they are? They are present as living beings filled with sensations, feelings, thoughts, images, desires, intentions. And in our lovemaking, are we not in fact *there* to one another, exposed, naked, visible in all aspects of our being in a way we both long for and fear? Are we not there for one another in a way that renounces the controlled, willful communication of speech, so that we are content to be and let be, to give what is asked and receive what is given? Is there not a hint here of union and presence, rather than simply a mutually enriching communication, and is not this hint of union and presence why it is so much easier to have a talk than it is to make love? All the personalists' talk about "talk" seems upon reflection a bit pale. It distorts the facts and removes the flavor from our lovemaking by destroying the language of unity, presence, and gift, and substituting for it the image of a mutually beneficial conversation between two autonomous individuals. In doing so, personalism diminishes us both in the complexity of our being and in the complexities of our relationships.

It is this diminishment of the full extent of our meeting in sexual relations that leads to a third difference between personalism and what for the moment I am calling "the other point of view." The two perceptions of what transpires in a sexual relation may produce very different reactions to adultery and premarital sex.

It is vital, indeed necessary, for us to have a number of social relations. It is particularly important for both personal and social health for men and women to be related one to another in many different ways. For this reason, we do carry on a number of conversations with other people—many of whom are of the opposite sex. These conversations are vehicles for many different forms of social exchange, and they involve our emotions and feelings. It is the great strength of personalism that it not only recognizes but commends these multifaceted and varied types of relationships between men and women. What is at issue, however, is not the many types of relation that take place between men and women, but whether or not a sexual relation is a morally right form of exchange if it takes place between men and women who are not husband and wife.

To be specific, if sex is understood as primarily a form of conversation intended for the mutual benefit of autonomous holders of rights and duties, rather than as a presentation and giving of some part of all that we are, it is not difficult to think of sexual engagements as being *limited* in duration and as appropriate with more than one partner at a time. After all, we can carry on a number of conversations at once, we can limit their duration and intensity, and we can hold conversations for a number of different purposes. In the case of personalism, the extensiveness and richness of the sexual exchange is limited from the start by the metaphor we use to grasp the nature of the engagement. If, however, the metaphor we use is one of unity, presence, and giving rather than talking, if we think of making love not as a limited exchange but as a form of self-presentation and self-giving that always promises a unity in which two become one, then we will, I think, find it more difficult to think of our sexual engagements as limited in respect to fidelity and permanence.

To put the point another way, on marking the difference between thinking of sexual relations as a form of conversation rather than as the primary mode of presence, self-giving, and unity, we must at least ask what our deep judgments are about the thought that the self-giving and self-exposure is only for the time being. We must ask as well what our judgments are about the thought that this sort of relation may be carried on with more than one woman or man at the same time. It is their diminished view of what happens in a sexual relation that makes it easier for personalists to flirt with temporary and multiple sexual relations, and to make these relations so univocally subservient to the personal needs of individuals. In contrast, a person who believes that the promise of a sexual relation is always the promise that two become "one flesh" will find it more difficult to accept a view that limits the significance of this form of exchange.

Perhaps this point can be given support and made concrete by asking about the nature of jealousy. Jealousy is a well-known and widespread passion, but its meaning and value are not always clear to us. It is illuminating, however, to ask how a personalist and an advocate of the other point of view respectively might be inclined to view and judge this nearly universal human reaction. Since their dominant analogies are the verbal one of conversation and the economic one of beneficial trade, personalists will almost certainly note that conversation, like trade, can be carried on with many people. From this perspective, jealousy will appear a rather selfish emotion. Perhaps the jealous partner even ought to feel guilty. Is it not selfish to begrudge one's beloved those other "conversations" necessary for growth and happiness? Perhaps we ought to be generous, so that our partner can escape the boredom of a conversation repeated for several years.

Without question, jealousy can be and perhaps most often is a sign of some lack of love. But is this ancient passion to be understood *only* as the expression of an uncertain and ungenerous spirit?

Suppose one sees a sexual relation as something more than a symbolic exchange between "persons." Suppose they see sex as the most intensive and extensive form of presence and exchange, a form of presence and self-giving that links them soul and body with another life. Suppose they think of a sexual relation as a form of giving and receiving that promises and effects a union of body and soul, as opposed to a mutually beneficial exchange between two autonomous individuals. From such a perspective, might they not see in a jealous reaction the expression of true love and commitment? Might not jealousy be viewed as a reaction that indicates the primal and sacred character of the relation and as an emotion that stands guard over a special relationship whose uniqueness ought to be kept, whose particularity ought not to be shared, and whose bond of unity is so close that it precludes the presence of third parties?

Jealousy often is an ungenerous reaction. It can, however, be the reaction of a faithful heart that is prepared to fight for the integrity of its closest relationship and to seek to protect it from perfidious alienation. A jealous lover may indeed be a leech. A lover incapable of jealousy, on the other hand, may be no lover at all.

It is the positive, indeed just, aspect of jealousy that made it possible for the emotion to be ascribed to the God of Israel. Jealousy is an emotion that is sparked by the disruptive and alienating intrusion of a third party into a relationship that in certain quite specific ways ought to be kept sacrosanct. Jealousy is a protective mechanism that warns both parties to a sexual relation that some threat to their union has appeared—a threat that quite rightly ought to be guarded against. We might even say that jealousy is a reaction which in some circumstances true lovers owe one another. If we look at jealousy in this way, we can understand why the phrase "I the Lord am a jealous God" runs throughout the Old Testament. God is Israel's lover and husband who betrothed her in her youth. As her husband, God insists that Israel forsake all other gods (rivals) and keep herself only for God. The view of marriage and sexual relation in Hosea 3 is like that in Genesis 1–3. Presence and fidelity are a part of God's intention for sexual relation.

It is exactly this faithfulness that Israel abandons. She takes other lovers—perhaps for her own self-fulfillment. God's reaction is not one of gentle tolerance, but jealous wrath. The righteous, jealous wrath of God is not, however, a sign of self-righteous and possessive weakness. It is the jealousy of God that shows both the depth of his feeling and the strength of his determination to guard and keep a relation that ought not to be violated. It is God's jealous love that leads him to insist that Israel put away her other lovers and keep herself only for her husband. Both the depth of God's love and the nature of the relationship demand this unequivocal fidelity. God and Israel are, in a way, "one flesh." Israel's infidelity tears at God's innards; it rips away at the very heart of God's life. The pain and outrage of God's jealousy is a measure of his love and righteousness.

Jealousy can be the reaction of a faithful love. It appears to be an emotion that seeks to keep third parties from intruding themselves into relationships in illicit and destructive ways. Furthermore, if human jealousy is transformed in our hearts, minds, and bodies by the faithful love that stands behind God's presence and self-giving to his bride, the church, that emotion will produce in us a similar determination to maintain the integrity of our sexual relations and it will suggest a different view of multiple or temporary liaisons. Jealousy may be a phenomenon that places the tolerant flirtations of personalism with multiple and impermanent sexual relations in a different light. We may see the possessive feelings we have about the one we love as a trace of God's intentions for our sexual relations, not simply as the grasping possessiveness of an ungenerous spirit.

2.

These observations, like the previous ones I have made, once again will not settle the issues the personalists raise about sexual relations, but they will lead those who look at sexual relations from the other point of view to be wary of what often appears as excessive tolerance—a tolerance they may suspect of masking a lack of love and a lack of seriousness about life's most intensive and extensive form of exchange.

Adultery and premarital sex will at a minimum appear from the two perspectives in a very different pattern of light and shade. Personalists are prepared to see a significant area of light. Some light may indeed appear, but from the other point of view we have identified, the shade cast by these relations will almost certainly cover a wider area than the light. Furthermore, the extensive area of shade that appears may even suggest the shadows of the garden in which the man and the woman hide from God because of their shame.

The wariness of those who view non-marital sexual relations from the other point of view will be increased by another factor that the previous image of light and shadow suggests. We have seen that in his account of origins, the Yahwist looks at sexual relations through two windows at the same time. One window [Gen. 2] provides a view of sexual relations as God intends them to be; the other [Gen.

3] overlooks a scene wherein the effects of the disobedience of the man and the woman appear. Among the effects is the distortion of the "one flesh" unity God intends. Because of their disobedience, the man and the woman are, in significant ways, always absent or hidden one from another. They must cover their nakedness. So also each now tends to place blame for their motives and actions elsewhere.

Hiddenness and self-deception weaken the unity of the man and the woman, and we must assume that both hiddenness and self-deception are carried into the struggle of dominance and subservience that further distorts the bond God intends to exist between them. Christians traditionally have seen in this account of disobedience the paradigmatic results of sin or the fall. The break with God brought about by the disobedience of *adam,* male and female (however that break is understood), results not only in the loss of God's immediate presence, but also in the loss of openness, honesty, and harmony in the relationships between the man and the woman.

If this narrative and the one contained in Genesis 2 shape our view of the relations that do obtain and ought to obtain between men and women, what reaction are we likely to have to impermanent or inclusive sexual relations? We will, I think, be forced to ask in a more pressing way than do the personalists if these relationships contain the sort of presence and self-giving they promise and invite. In this respect, we will be led to ask quite specific questions about the openness and honesty of such relations. We will have to ask these questions because our paradigmatic account of the relation between the man and the woman speaks not only of the relation's intended blessings, but also of the dishonesty and self-interest that now so infect and threaten it. The Genesis account of the relation between the man and the woman, in fact, provides a means to grasp both the promise of sexual relationships and the threats to their health and integrity.

If viewed from the perspective of either promise or threat, sexual relations outside of marriage appear problematic. Similarly, the traditional Christian insistence on fidelity and permanence become more intelligible and more humane. Both can be seen as providing necessary conditions for the sort of presence and self-giving sexual relations promise and demand. Both also can be seen to protect sexual relations from their most dangerous enemies—deception and dominance. To be specific, it is fidelity and permanence that provide a necessary counter-balance to the hidden motives, self-deceptions, desires for dominance, and temptations toward self-betrayal that stand ever ready to delay or render forfeit the promise contained in sexual relations. If we view sexual relations from the perspective of Genesis 2 and 3, we will be able to see that fidelity and permanence provide a barrier reef that protects them from the inrush of tides that can easily unmoor us. Fidelity and permanence provide restraints upon our motives and acts, and at the same time bring to light our selfish tendencies toward the abuse and deception of those we love. Precisely because there is no easy way out, we find ourselves in a position where speaking the truth both about the one we love and about ourselves becomes a possibility. Fidelity and permanence provide the time and space for lovers to meet and know one another, an opportunity to learn whether or not we are able to recognize, point out, and forgive the deception and injuries that are bound to be part of all our relationships, and whether we can love the other as the person they are and not as the image of our dreams and projections.

At their best, Christians have understood that fidelity and permanence not only show forth forgivenesss, but provide space and time for it to come about. Fidelity and permanence thus inscribe a circle in which reconciliation can occur, and so also an arena in which we can struggle to put off our old self-interested and deceptive nature and, in Paul's words, "put on a new nature." It is this new nature that allows us to love this particular neighbor, my wife or my husband, as we love ourselves—that is, as our own flesh.

Fidelity and permanence are thus necessary for the fulfillment of the promise contained in sexual relations, as well as for the protection of these relations from the forces that threaten them. Finally, they are necessary if our sexual relations are to be brought into Christ and so fulfilled in the deepest sense we can know or imagine. This brings us to the brink of yet another outlook on the nature and purpose of sexual relations. Our stories suggest that our sexual relations reflect both our created and our fallen nature. Do they carry any meaning for those who have "put on" Christ? Do they play any part in God's plan for the redemption or salvation of the world?

Christians traditionally have said they do, and once again the vision that stands behind such a claim will lead to suspicion of anything less than unqualified fidelity and permanence. For it is a vision of the nature of salvation that has led Christians to say that sexual relations are "right" and "good" in an unqualified sense only when they take place between people who have made vows that they will give themselves sexually *only* to one another until parted by death. The classical text for such a vision is Ephesians 5:21–33. It is this passage that provides the final source of the other point of view for which we have been searching; it is the most basic and comprehensive statement concerning how it is that one may be many and yet many one. For the author of the Epistle to the Ephesians, God's plan from before the creation has been to unite all things in himself in and through the life, death, and resurrection of Christ. God's plan to unite all things is revealed in Christ, but it is the church that makes known this mystery and lives it out in its common life. Unexpectedly, the relation that most adequately represents God's plan for unity is that between husband and wife. In their union of "one flesh" we see the most complete expression possible of Christ's relation to the church and of the relation one to another of the members of the church, the most adequate expression we have of how God in Christ intends that one be many and yet many one.

A quick look at the basic argument of the epistle will

make clear the meaning of what I have said. The author opens with a statement about God's plan "for the fullness of time." This plan, also called the "mystery of his will," has been revealed and accomplished in Christ. The "plan" or "mystery" is to unite all things in Christ [1:19]. The reason for the plan is to bring all creation to praise God's glory and so to its appointed end and fulfillment. We who are many become one with God and with each other in Christ. We are, in the mystery of God's will, brought to a new life. This life comes about by grace through faith and the presence of God's spirit [1:13; 2:8]. It is this life, in which many have become one in Christ, that is our destiny and inheritance. It is also our hope [1:10].

It is within the context of God's plan that the author of Ephesians understood his own life. He was appointed to make this plan known to the Gentiles [3:1]. By grace through faith, the mystery of God's will was both preached and believed. As a result, God's plan, which will be fulfilled in the resurrected life, begins to take effect in the present one. Those who are many because of sin are through Christ's sacrifice on the cross reconciled to God and one another. As the hostility between God and *adam* is put to an end, so too is the hostility between Jew and Gentile. The wall between them is broken down. Together they become a new *adam*— one body, fellow members of a household, fellow citizens, a holy temple which is the dwelling place on earth of God's spirit [2:17–22]. Those who were one in God in creation, but became many through sin, are now made one once again in Christ.

This is the message of the epistle, the good news Christians are to proclaim and live out. They have been appointed or destined to do so not only to enjoy the new life God gives, but also make this life known. In what the body of believers is, says, and does, the mystery is made visible.

For this reason, all who believe are to give up their old way of life, in which they were led by selfishness into division, hostility, uncleanness, and mendacity. In the new life of love and of unity hostility is replaced by peace, and each member of Christ's body is related to the other members in a particular way. Each is now to the other a gift rather than an enemy through a presence and self-giving like that of Christ himself. The many become one in Christ through the grace of God's sacrifice and forgiveness, and this act of grace calls forth in the church an imitation. The body of the new *adam*, it is called and instructed to imitate God, to walk in love as Christ did [5:1–2]. In following this call, the many become one and yet, because each has a particular gift, remain many.

In Christ all things reach their appointed destiny and fulfillment; they participate in the mystery of the divine life.

The fulfillment of God's plan comes about in part through the witness and common life of the church. The central example of this fulfillment, however, is its most intimate and domestic expression. To our surprise, the mystery of God's will may be most clearly seen in domestic relations between husbands and wives, parents and children, masters and slaves. Of these relations, that between husband and wife is most fit to signify and make known the divine plan. It has more power than any other to make known and effect God's will for all things. This relation is the crucial one wherein we are to be imitators of God and so walk in love.

How is such love to be expressed? We are to be *subject* one to another. The subjection we owe, however, is out of reverence for Christ. With some boldness one may say, I think, that it is like that between Father, Son, and Holy Spirit. Such a qualification is crucial because mutual subjection, the key to how many become one in a new way, is always defined by Christ's love and sacrifice for us, and so by God's own life. Walking in love or mutual subjection is Christomorphic and finally Trinitarian; on earth, the forms it takes will differ according to the relationship in question. In the body of the church, each offers and receives gifts to and from one another; in the household, more specific determinations are needed, but presence and self-giving are to shape the relation. Between parents and children, subjection implies honor and obedience from children, and forbearance, instruction, and the discipline of Christ from parents. With slaves, it will take the form of obedience and good will; with masters, forbearance.

Within the household, the mystery is to take effect and be visible through transformed relations of mutual subjection. Nowhere is this transformation more visible than in the relation between husband and wife. Wives are required to be "subject" to their husbands; such a charge, like the ones to children and slaves, jars our modern ears and in many ways it should. Our author's instructions for walking in love are indeed both hierarchical and patriarchal. Love and mutual subjection have been refracted through the prism of the cultural forms of the day, and this refraction reflects a bygone social structure. If we think a moment, however, we will realize that the author's account of mutual subjection transforms that ancient social structure with its hierarchical domestic relations almost beyond recognition.

Despite our initial impressions to the contrary, Ephesians' account of walking in love and mutual subjection is transformative rather than conservative. We can see this in the limits love places on subjection, respect, and honor, and by the definition it gives the "superior" position of husband, parent, and master. The "superior" position of each simply carries with it a greater responsibility for the transformation of the relation in question. For example, although the wife is to be subject to and respect her husband, she is to do so *only* as to the Lord. This she cannot do if her husband's treatment of her is not like Christ's treatment of the church. If his love and care of her is not of this nature, the wife cannot be subject "as to the Lord." Thus, the husband, like Christ, is to give himself up for his wife. His "superiority" (if superiority is indeed the right word) has become one of sacrifice.

In making such a sacrifice the husband shows both his love for God and Christ and for his neighbor. He is thus made one with both, as God intends. The husband in his sacrifice does not put an end to hierarchy, but he does put an end to the rule and domination of Genesis 3. Whatever giving up oneself as Christ gave himself means, it means an end to domination. It means also that in loving his wife as Christ loved the church, the husband fulfills not only the first but the second commandment. He not only loves God, but loves his neighbor as himself.

His wife, after all, is "one flesh" with him. They are one in and through their sexual relation. Thus, in loving his wife, the husband loves her "as he loves himself," and whatever he wishes for himself now becomes the criterion for judging what he gives his wife. What is to be given is in this case, as in all cases, determined by the nature of Christ's presence and self-giving. Only in this context can the wife's charge to be "subject" be understood. The hierarchical relation between husband and wife remains, but not the dominance. These are replaced by mutual subjection out of reverence for Christ. In our modern egalitarian age, we must further imagine that the subjection demanded of the wife will resemble that demanded of the husband. She also is to care as Christ cares for the church, and to give herself up.

Here in microcosm God's plan is signified, and here in miniature it becomes a present reality. Two become one in a new way—in the way defined by God himself. They are united with God and with one another in Christ, and so walk in love and mutual subjection. Thus *adam*, male and female, are once again "image of God," and so they signify to us as well the relation between Christ and the church. Their relation displays God's life, and so the heart of God's plan, the mystery of his will, to save us by making us one with him and with one another. It has this power because it is the only relation that permits presence and self-giving in all their forms. Sex, money, power, and language are all involved. What better metaphor could we find for how the many are to become one, which catches up all dimensions of human life and society? It is this relation that recapitulates all forms of exchange or communication, and so signifies our unity and division as no other can.

If we view sexual relations through this prism, then, how will an openness to multiple or temporary sexual relations appear? Even the insistence that openness to other sexual relations requires responsibility, care, love, trust, and openness should make us suspicious. Each of these virtues begins to sound in the mouths of many of their users highly qualified, and certainly as something less than the love, responsibility, care, trust, and openness manifest in Christ's giving up of himself for the church. Many contemporary presentations of fidelity and permanence will also seem disturbingly hedged about with qualifiers. We will wonder if, with such a qualified love, *the man* and *the woman* love their partner as themselves, and we will certainly wonder if the love they show is like the love Christ shows for the church.

Once again, the window through which we view a scene shapes what we see of its pattern of light and shade. If we view sexual relations from the perspective of the Epistle to the Ephesians, which insists that they are destined to be caught up in the mystery of God's life and God's saving purpose, signifying this mystery as no other relations can, non-marital sexual relations will appear far more problematic to us that they do to the ears of modern personalists—even Christian ones. I am convinced that if we view impermanent, temporary sexual relations from the other point of view I have sketched, the personalist case will begin to appear for what it is—yet another example of the atomistic individualism of our age. From behind the rhetoric of relationship, and out of the moral fog of highly qualified moral terms, will appear the acquisitive and isolated ego of modern consciousness.

When the dust has settled, the church will, I believe, continue to hold out for real sex instead of its revisionist imposters. Beside the "one flesh" unity sex promises and to which Christians have pointed, the individually focused and timid exchanges proposed in most revisionist sexual ethics will appear as the shady deals that more often than not they are. In order that real sex, with all the fullness of its promise, may be distinguished from its counterfeits, and the "one flesh" union of *the man* and *the woman* retain its power to display the divine mystery, the church will continue to insist for both pastoral and evangelistic reasons that sexual relations ought to take place *only* between a man and a woman who have made a covenant to be faithful one to another until parted by death.

In the end, such a hard-nosed defense of real sex will prove both loving toward the neighbor and obedient to God. Such, it seems to me, is the implication of the primary metaphor ("and the two become one flesh") that Christians have until now used to grasp the nature and promise of our sexual engagements.

The question remains whether the churches will continue to explore in their moral reflection the meaning of this metaphor, or whether in their attempt to become again the moral arbiters of an entire society they will adopt another— that of free and open trading between free and essentially unrelated "persons." The popularity which James Nelson's personalist sexual ethics has enjoyed among the clergy of the major denominations suggests that the temptation to change our major metaphor to an individualistic and highly economic one is enormous. The major denominations may indeed make such a change in order to accommodate more easily the varied interests of their respective constituencies. In order to maintain their place in an atomistic, contractarian society, they will be tempted to give up the metaphors that stand in starkest judgment on the basic assumptions of their surrounding culture. In respect to sex, money, power and language, the great temptation of the denominations will be to offer a new religious charter for the atomism and essential selfishness of the age.

WEALTH, POVERTY AND TRUTH

It is not money that is the root of all evil, but the human heart. The gnomic saying about money and evil with which we are all familiar is, in fact, false, but money is nonetheless a fearfully powerful reality. It may even have more power over our imaginations than sex.

A good case can be made for saying that the dominant metaphors of our age are economic. We speak of "owning" a particular point of view. Americans express their agreement by saying, "I'll buy that." William Safire pointed out recently that economic language now dominates even our political vocabulary. We are, he said, increasingly loath to speak of principles. We prefer to speak of "values." Behind this change in usage lies a shift in political understanding of enormous significance. Safire points out that

> the Latin *principium* meant "source, origin, beginning." That came to mean a primary truth that formed the basis for other beliefs and then to mean a rule for ethical conduct.

The origins of the term "value" are quite different. Its root is the Latin word for strength, and the plural meant what value came to mean in English—material worth. Safire's point is that while principles abide, values are impermanent. Value is like money; its worth fluctuates with the forces of the market. In Safire's words, principles

> are fixed, invariable, absolute, eternal. . . . Values, being in a sense scientific, are nontheological and therefore subject to change and alteration as the demands and needs of a society change.[24]

Safire laments the change in our political vocabulary from principle to value. I join him in his sorrow, but for the moment my purpose is simply to note that this shift from principle to value has taken place not just in politics, but throughout our moral vocabulary, and as a consequence, economic metaphors now dominate our moral discourse and our moral imagination. We calculate the relative value of our acts and practices as we balance our bank accounts. We try not so much to do the truth, but to see that our actions have "profitable" results. Because of the metaphors we use, we understand the moral life more and more as a matter of profit and loss. Money is not the root of all evil, but for us it provides a primary metaphor for grasping our basic engagements. Money has a hold not only on our desires but on our minds; it fuels the imagination as well as moves the heart.

It is ironic that in an age whose imagination is fired by "value" rather than truth, beauty or goodness, money should have such a small place in the realm of personal ethics. It is even more ironic that the place money now occupies in Christian moral discourse has shrunk more and more. Greed was once considered a serious vice and generosity a laudable virtue. These virtues and vices were not thought to be matters of private taste alone. Society had an interest in encouraging virtue and inhibiting vice; parents, teachers, priests and pastors took an interest in moral education. Both church and society thought it wise to raise questions about our acquisitive desires and practices and to offer models for escaping the clutches of what often became a destructive power—the love of money.

It now appears that both within society as a whole and within the major denominations, the question of money is becoming more and more a private affair. Debate still rages, to be sure, around the moral acceptability of economic systems and the redistribution of wealth, but money as an object of desire, as a personal possession and as an influence over the imagination hardly receives comment. In many ways money, like sex, has become a matter of taste. There are voices, to which I would like to add my own, that wish to reintroduce the subjects of virtue and vice into moral discourse, but this is not the place for it.[25] My concern at the moment has more to do with the disposition of money in society. It is not, however, in the first instance a concern about public policy, but rather one about the ordering of monetary relations within the church.

To begin, I simply wish to note the contrary direction of most Christian social ethics. In an age when monetary images have so thoroughly captured the mind of the public, Christian ethicists, like their secular counterparts, have chosen to focus their attention on economic systems and upon the redistribution of wealth. Little attention has been given to those practices that ought to order the distribution and disposal of wealth within the Christian community. Thus questions of virtue and of the form of life within the church have been eclipsed by a debate over economic systems and public policy.

The Constantinian settlement is coming unraveled, but the Constantinian dream lives on. By raising questions about economic systems and policies, both liberal and conservative neo-Constantinians hope to do more than contribute to a public debate. They hope to reassert the church's role as moral arbiter for an entire society. The Roman Catholic bishops seem quite self-conscious about what is going on. They

are openly Constantinian, and in their pastoral letter on Roman Catholic social teaching and the U.S. economy are, according to one report in the New York Times, knowingly
"moving into what they consider the vacuum left by the
decline of moral influence of the mainline Protestant
churches."[26]

It is, I grant, naughty but still true to say that Jerry
Falwell is competing for the same territory. It is by now
obvious that my contention is that neither the Catholic bishops, nor the National Council of Churches, nor Jerry Falwell
will succeed, and that all are ignoring the first concern of
Christian social ethics in respect to money. How is the distribution and disposal of money within the church to be
ordered?

The result of this oversight is more far-reaching than
most of us realize. It produces two baleful results. The first
is that the denominations jettison the real chance they have,
through the witness of their common lives, to exert moral
influence on our economic system. The second is even more
serious: their proclamation of the Christian gospel lacks
power. If the first task of Christian social ethics is the constitution of the church, and if one of the primary purposes
Christians have for the moral enterprise is the display of the
truth they proclaim, then for Christians the moral life is a
matter of "practicing what they preach," so that what they
preach may be seen and believed.

To put the matter somewhat bluntly, Christian social
ethics is connected with evangelism: the proclamation of the
Christian gospel involves not only speaking, but also doing
the truth, and both of these activities take place in the most
fundamental way within the fellowship of the church. What
Christians *do* among themselves in respect to sex, money,
power and speech is part and parcel of what they have to
say, both to themselves and to the world, about God.

Money is always a good test for finding where the heart
is and in this instance it provides as well an excellent issue
with which to test my premise. I say this in part because

"liberation theology"—the one form of Christian social ethics that has in recent years taken money with the seriousness it deserves—has related the mission of the church so closely to the alteration of economic systems. I do not wish to imply that liberation theologians have given no attention to the disposal of wealth in the church, but only that their first concern has been society. They are, furthermore, so suspicious of "charity" that on occasion one wonders if they do not oppose it altogether. For these and other reasons, I believe they not only misconstrue the first task of Christian social ethics, but also fail to make clear and recommend with power the gospel of the church.

It is more adequate, I think, to hold that Christians are called first to live out a new form of life whose primary purpose is religious. It is to lead more deeply into the life of God, give expression to God's love for his people, and to display that love for all to see and believe. The new way of life to which Christians are called can and ought to provide images with which to view the life of society as a whole, models for its transformation and the motive, power and skill to undertake it. To test this thesis, I propose to investigate one particular issue—the relation between wealth, the remedy of poverty, and evangelism. By providing another point of view than that of the liberation theologians, I hope both to defend my thesis and indicate a way ahead for Christian social ethics in a "post-Constantinian" age.

The primary outlines of liberation theology are well known. I wish only to sketch these lines insofar as they bear upon wealth, poverty and the mission of the church. Gustavo Gutierrez' *A Theology of Liberation* is still the basic and most comprehensive text of the liberationist school and will serve to illustrate their point of view. Gutierrez has undertaken a sophisticated and provocative reconstruction of Christian belief that he hopes will make the Christian gospel meaningful in a world that has (a) lived through the enlightenment (wherein "man" is thought to take charge of his destiny upon earth) and (b) has become hideously divided between oppressed and oppressing classes of people and nations. Gutierrez' thesis is that history may be understood by following two converging lines of development. One line starts from the fact that "man" is self-creating and, as such, has charge of his own destiny. The other is that God, with the cooperation of "man," moves all history toward a fulfillment Christians know as the kingdom of God.

According to Gutierrez, these two lines of growth are not identical, but they are coincident; they ought neither to be separated nor confused. For Gutierrez true self-creation works toward fuller humanity, and so toward a society in which there is peace, justice, love and liberty. The kingdom of God includes these developments, but is more than their sum. The kingdom is, like human self-creation, an historical reality, but one that is to achieve not only human growth, but also the conquest of sin. This makes possible life's fulfillment—a state in which all people love God and one another. In a final sense, God's kingdom is God's gift; only God can conquer sin and bring about such love. But the divine gift does not take place apart from the human work of "co-creation," wherein social, economic and political structures that are more just, more loving, more peaceful and more liberating are brought about.

Thus, according to Gutierrez, the socio-economic activity of people is, if it accords with the fraternal life of peace, justice, love and freedom to which all people are destined, an aspect of salvation. In consequence, there is no real separation between secular history and salvation history.

How do we know the destiny to which we are called? It has been made known in the life, death and resurrection of Jesus. In his life the future is revealed and the divine plan made manifest. In Christ, all things are united in that he loved God, he loved his neighbors as himself, and so identified with the oppressed (the poor) and stood against the powerful.

What then is the mission of the church? It is to proclaim the good news of the kingdom of God. The church cannot fulfill this mission, however, without identifying with the poor and engaging in evangelism that is politically instructive. History is growth toward the kingdom of God; it moves toward the complete rule of God in history. Nevertheless, this same history involves class struggle. If the church is to remain faithful to its mission, it must side with the poor against the rich—with the oppressed against their oppressors.

What then is the church? It is more than the baptized. Grace works everywhere. There are "anonymous Christians," many of whom may be atheists. Whoever joins the struggle against oppression and for peace, justice, love and freedom is in the sphere of grace, just as those who oppose these movements are in the sphere of sin. The true church is not bounded by ecclesial walls nor defined by baptism, but composed of those who identify with the goal of human self-creation and with God's purposes for his kingdom. This being so, what is the role of the institution we call the church? For our purposes this is the basic question and we may now attempt an answer.

The institutional church is called to be a "sacrament."[27] In making this statement, Gutierrez cites Colossians 1:26 and in so doing uses the notion in its original sense to refer not to the sacraments of baptism and eucharist, but to the fulfillment and manifestation of God's plan of salvation. The fulfillment of this plan is the creation of "koinonia," a fellowship where there is love for God and love for our neighbors manifested in three strategic dimensions of unity—the sharing of goods, the fellowship of believers in the eucharist, and a union of love with God the Father.

At first glance Gutierrez' proposal for Christian social ethics looks something like the very one advocated here. Nevertheless, one waits in vain for an explication of what the implications of "koinonia" might be for the common life of the church. He makes no more than passing mention of fraternal relations within the body of the church and the sharing of goods, and then begins a discussion of the calling of the institutional church to become a political force and to throw its weight behind the cause of the poor. To say that the church is a sacrament means for Gutierrez that the mission of the church as an institution has a political dimension. The institution is to give support to causes, reforms, parties, proposals, candidates, and revolutionary armies (we are never told exactly which) that favor the cause of the poor against the rich.

Accordingly, the conflict fought out politically in society is not to be lived out *differently* in the church, but continued within it. The class struggle rages both within and without, and the institution must not avoid it. The church is called to denounce injustice and announce the goal of human history. It is to side with those whom God favors—the poor. The church then is a sacrament primarily in the sense that it is to back the political forces that favor the poor. Gutierrez is even prepared to admit that what he advocates is "a Constantinianism of the left," even if this means the continuation of the class struggle within the body of the church.[28]

There are, I believe, many difficulties with the position Gutierrez articulates, but my purpose is not to enter a thoroughgoing criticism. I cite Gutierrez for the positive reason that he takes money seriously, recognizing that the subject cannot be avoided if we are to talk in any meaningful way about the mission of the church or Christian social ethics. He recognizes the connection between wealth, poverty and the truth about God that Christians are sent to proclaim and live out. He knows full well the importance of defining what poverty really is and by Biblical exegesis tries to find an answer. What does his exegesis reveal and how adequate is it?

After reviewing the relevant Biblical material, he concludes that poverty is an "ambiguous" term. I think his choice of the term "ambiguous" is misleading and will try to show why, but still he is aware of the fact that in the Bible poverty is not a simple notion. It means first of all material poverty— a lack of those goods necessary for a life worthy of the name human. Such poverty is not pictured in the Bible as having a positive value; it is, in fact, degrading. Nor, according to the biblical witness, is it a matter of fate. People are not destined to be poor, but are poor because of sin and injustice.

> The existence of poverty represents a sundering both of solidarity among men and also of communion with God. Poverty is an expression of sin, that is, of a negation of love. It is, therefore, incompatible with the coming of the Kingdom of God, a Kingdom of love and justice.[29]

The second meaning of poverty, according to Gutierrez, is humility. It is also "the ability to welcome God, an openness to God, a willingness to be used by God, a humility before God."[30] Poverty is opposed to pride, and so becomes synonymous with faith or trust. Like faith, poverty is a precondition for a relation with God. We might say that the biblical witness about wealth and poverty is that we are all beggars before God.

According to Gutierrez, poverty in the Bible also has a third meaning, for it can be understood as well as "a commitment of solidarity and protest." Just as Christ became poor for our sake, so the church is to proclaim humility and self-sacrifice. The proclamation of both entails solidarity with the poor and protest against the injustice that keeps them poor. It follows, Gutierrez believes, that in today's world acts of love, liberation, solidarity and protest entail political action on behalf of the oppressed and against the oppressors. That poverty entails political commitment is, to Gutierrez, fundamental to its meaning.

Gutierrez' analysis of the meaning of poverty is one that has much to recommend it. It is not helpful, however, to say that in the Bible the meaning of poverty is "ambiguous." It is complex, but not ambiguous. It is better to say that in the Bible the meaning of poverty is multifaceted, open-textured, or polyvalent. Each of the several meanings flows into the other; each is connected with the others and each is present whenever the word is used, even if attention is focused on one sense rather than the others. It is because Gutierrez does not give sufficient attention to the interconnections between the various senses of poverty that he sometimes separates the various meanings, and at the same time focuses undue attention on material poverty and on the political commitment on behalf of the poor against the rich.

But let us look more carefully at the biblical meaning of poverty and see how adequate his case is. I believe that as its inadequacies are revealed, another point of view will emerge—one that gives a more adequate account of the interconnections between wealth, poverty and the truth Christians are sent to proclaim. It is indeed true, as Gutierrez says, that "the poor" is a classification with several meanings in the Bible. In the Old Testament the poor are those who do not have the means (often land or familial connections) to obtain life's most basic necessities—food, clothing and shelter—and who find themselves in debt and in danger of falling into slavery. This marginal state leaves the poor without the ability to help or defend themselves. They are vulnerable to exclusion from the benefits of covenant society and to exploitation by wealthy and powerful people. Thus "the poor" are defined not only by economic criteria, but by social and political criteria as well. Their vulnerability opens the way for the second use of the term poverty—a use Gutierrez also identifies. Because the poor are vulnerable, marginal and alienated, they come to be thought of also as those people whose hope is rooted solely in the faithfulness, mercy and power of God. They can count neither upon their own strength nor upon that of an earthly redeemer or savior. Their hope, quite literally, is "in the name of the Lord."

This sense of the term "the poor" supports Gutierrez' contention that "the poor" are those who have the ability to "welcome God." Gutierrez is right to link poverty and piety in this way but he does not sufficiently reveal their interconnection. He obscures the fact that material and spiritual poverty are always paired notions. Neither meaning can be employed without carrying the other along. One can see their linkage with particular clarity in the psalms, where typically it is the poor who call out for divine help and vindication against their oppressors. The state of the poor throws them into the arms of God, just as the state of the rich and powerful drives them to rely upon themselves, reject God, and exploit the poor. Material and spiritual poverty are not *two* kinds of poverty.

The polyvalent character of the term continues into the time of Jesus and its open-textured quality finds expression in the New Testament texts.[31] Thus "the poor" in the Lukan beatitudes and "the poor" depicted in the birth narratives are not two different sorts of poor people. In both instances they are people who are both "poor" and "pious." Gutierrez' interpretation divides these into two senses, and by seeking specific denotations for the terms, he too severely strips away their connotations.[32]

We have now posed and answered the first question: what is poverty and who are "the poor"? We may now ask the second: what is poverty's remedy? If the New Testament witness is to be believed, and if by remedy we mean "elimination," then God and only God can ultimately remedy the situation of the poor. Their final deliverance will be accomplished neither by themselves nor by any other human agent. As to how God provides this final remedy, the answer seems to be by establishing his rule. In the kingdom of God, poverty in both its material and spiritual sense will be eliminated. God will judge the peoples of the earth, and in so doing brings about a great reversal in which the pious/poor are raised up and the rich/impious are thrown down. A new community comes into being and inhabits a new earth whose fruits are abundant and ample. Both injustice and privation cease.

It must be emphasized again, however, that this new community and new earth come from God through a cataclysmic reversal initiated from beyond history. It does not evolve from below, as a number of Protestant thinkers from the time of Kant have suggested, and it is not (as the Marxists suggest) the simple product of the interplay of historical forces. Further, it is not (as Gutierrez suggests) the end product of a process of "growth." There is, to be sure, a connection between the course of history and the coming of the kingdom of God, but there is also a gap that cannot be bridged from the side of history.

The central witness of the New Testament is that God alone will eliminate poverty. The insistence of the New Testament writers on "inbreak" rather than "growth" is a necessary aspect of their belief in the sovereignty of God, the triumph of grace and the power of sin in human history. Unlike Gutierrez, they do not regard the human race as "co-creators" but as dishonest servants who have made something of a mess of the Lord's vineyard. Gutierrez' call for us to take charge of our own destiny and to become "co-creators" might sound to Paul and the evangelists like a call for us in both evolution and history to play God before we have learned to be men.[33] The cry of the New Testament writers was "Come, Lord Jesus." To pray for the elimination of poverty and injustice would have, for them, meant to pray "Thy Kingdom come." Their prayer was for the final appearance of God rather than for the end of a period of growth or the successful completion of a political struggle, so that their suffering would be foreshortened and their rest and bliss complete.

In the Lukan beatitudes, the focus is on material poverty, but Matthew's version reverses the emphasis. In the Matthean text, the notion of piety dominates that of poverty. The blessed of the Kingdom are the poor *in spirit* and those who hunger and thirst for righteousness. The Matthean text contains a distinct spiritualization of the notion of poverty, although it certainly does not eliminate poverty's most immediate meaning. Nevertheless, poverty's meaning takes a definite inward shift—opens the way for a proleptic enjoyment of foretaste of life in the kingdom. This foretaste, the early Christians knew, did not involve the elimination of poverty, but it did carry with it a release from poverty's destructive *power*. According to Matthew, those who are poor in spirit are free to "consider the lilies of the field," and they are admonished to "lay up treasures in heaven" that cannot, like earthly possessions, be lost. The poor in spirit possess what may be called an "inner freedom." Their trust in God, coupled with the obedience of true disciples, has proved for them protection against the harmful effect of both wealth and poverty. Gutierrez is correct when he claims that by the poor in spirit Matthew meant those who are "totally at the disposition of God,"[34] but he does not point out that this disposition gives a unique sort of freedom. The poor in spirit are inwardly free from both wealth and poverty. Gutierrez is loath to make this point, I believe, because he fears it will be used as an excuse to do nothing about the remedy of material poverty upon earth.

His fear is not without grounds, but it does not vitiate the conclusions about inner freedom that must be drawn from the Sermon on the Mount. A similar conclusion is found also in the writings of Paul, where the inner freedom of Christians is presented with relentless persistence. Through faith in the power of God revealed in Christ's death and resurrection, believers now have their lives centered in a new place. Their life is "hid" with God; though "penniless," they "own the world." Nothing can separate the believer from the love of God in Christ Jesus—not even poverty or riches.

I should like to illustrate the importance of this particular remedy for poverty by telling a story—a bit of my own biography—that took place on the day John Kennedy was shot.[35] I had accompanied the then Archbishop of Uganda on a confirmation trip, which took us to a small cattle camp on the banks of the Nile River about sixty miles north of Lake Victoria. The day was long and hot, the service was interminable, and then there were speeches and a huge feast. The festivities went on into the evening. We had gathered around a fire to sing hymns, and I remember being glad I was seated by the fire because it kept the mosquitoes away.

The singing went on and on. Just when I thought it would never stop, an old woman got up from her place near the back of the circle of people around the fire and began to walk slowly toward the bishop and myself. Stopping just in front of us, she raised her hand above her head. In it she held a gnarled and highly polished root all twisted round itself in a circle. The root was about the size of a grapefruit and it shimmered in the light of the fire. It was an eerie thing.

After a moment she said in a strong voice, "Jesus lives! Burn it!" Then she handed the root to the Archbishop and he threw it into the fire.

What she gave the Archbishop was a fetish thought to hold a spirit of great power—a spirit by means of which the old woman could bless or curse, kill or give life. She had paid over one hundred dollars for it; in her circumstances, a small fortune. She had given her life to obtain this thing and the power it gave her.

"Jesus lives! Burn it!" This exclamation was the old woman's version of Paul's "Penniless, we own the world." Her act expresses the inner freedom to which I refer as well as anything else I know.

If we dare conflate what are, no doubt, differing strains of thought, we can say that poverty in all its senses is ultimately remedied by God through the establishment of his kingdom, but that a proleptic, though partial, remedy is available through faith, which comes through the preaching of the gospel and the power of God's Spirit. Faith sets the believer free from the destructive power of both poverty and wealth. This freedom liberates us not only from the power of external, but also internal, forces that might separate us from God. To believers no final harm may come, no matter what enemies they face. In this way the great eschatological reversal whereby the poor become rich and rich become poor (Dives and Lazarus) is made a present, though inner, reality.

I suspect that though many will not wish to deny what has been said to this point, they will nevertheless find themselves somewhat uncomfortable. Their discomfort may come more from what has not been said than from what has. A question hovers about. Is it true that all Christians have to do for the poor is witness to the victory of God? Does this exhaust Christian obligation? Can believers be satisfied, pure and simple, with inner freedom?

I wish to argue, against the secular consciousness that seems to me more and more to dominate the mind of America's mainline denominations, that though there is much more that Christians have to say and do in respect to poverty and its remedy, they ought nevertheless not to despise the notion of inner freedom. There is no reason for Christians to accept the Marxist view that such talk serves merely as an opiate to dull the consciousness of the people. Though they hope for more, Christians certainly ought to be satisfied with nothing *less* than "inner freedom" and hope in the coming of God's kingdom. Though genuine faith, hope and love will lead Christians to attempts to remedy the sufferings of the poor and the conditions that bring their sufferings about, they nonetheless ought not to identify the hope that is within them with the improvement of individual or social conditions. To make such an identification is to trade their birthright for a mess of pottage.

Given the present climate within the denominations, it seems to me essential to enter such cautionary remarks. In view of the growing strength of the Christian right, it is also essential to insist that something more is required of Christians than the proclamation of God's victory and the promise of "inner freedom." The New Testament speaks of other dimensions of the remedy of poverty, and these too are necessary expressions of faith, hope and love. I am speaking of the help believers owe to one another, and particularly to the poor in their midst, which even a cursory reading of the New Testament presents. The faith by which one enters the kingdom of God, if it is indeed faith, produces works, and among these relief of the poor is of major importance. Put slightly differently, the law of love which governs life in the

kingdom of God requires, among other things, an attempt
to relieve the poverty of one's neighbor. Care of the poor,
particularly the poor among one's fellow believers, was
thought to signify one aspect of the proclamation of God's
victory over sin and death. Unbelievers could see in these
works of love the power of God, and so be presented with
the possibility of belief in the church's proclamation.

While there is still time, believers are to do good to all
people and especially to those who are of the household of
faith. Such claims are found throughout the New Testament,
particularly in the gospel of Luke. The obligation of Christians with means toward their poor brothers and sisters is
so strong that each congregation ought to be a community
in which poverty, in the sense of extreme material privation,
is remedied now, on earth.[36] To be sure, Luke's classification
"the poor" includes more than the destitute of the church,
as the parable of the Good Samaritan makes clear, yet he is
particularly anxious to picture Christian congregations as
communities in which those who have means contribute to
the relief of the poor among their fellow believers. This obligation included the poor of other congregations as well
(Acts 11:12–30). Indeed, the obligation to help the poor of
the church is so strong, Luke believes, that among Christians
there ought to be no needy people (Acts 4:32–39).

Paul's views are similar. Through faith believers are incorporated into "one body" held together in love. So close
is the new relation of believers in one body or family that if
one suffers, all suffer (I Cor. 12:26). Accordingly Paul is
shocked to find that at the family's common meal, while one
is hungry, another is drunk. So also he insists that Gentile
Christians contribute to relieve the poverty of the Jewish
Christians in Jerusalem. In Paul, as in Luke, one finds the
same insistence that the poor of one's own and other congregations be cared for. To return to a previous theme, the
exchange that takes place within the church between the rich
and the poor is a central aspect of the way in which many
become one, yet remain many. The care Christians owe and

give one another is a manifestation of the mystery of the plan of God to unite all things in Christ Jesus. In the new family money, like sex, becomes a vehicle for the proclamation and demonstration of God's love and of his power over sin and death. To bypass the poor brother or sister on the way to a political act, as the liberationists tend to do, is to pass by the poor Christ in our midst and so obscure the truth he made known and lived out.

Both Paul and Luke believe that Christians are to make special efforts to remedy the economic and social position of the poor among their own company, acts of love that both express and proclaim God's love for us and the love God's mercy calls forth. For these reasons, evangelism and the remedy of poverty among Christians are inextricably tied together. Abuses and temptations connected with the care of the poor were not thought by Paul or the other New Testament writers to vitiate the fundamental obligation of Christians to show forth the new life of the kingdom of God through transformed monetary and social relations within the church. Paul and Luke would, I think, feel the same way today. The inevitable abuses of the poor by the rich and the rich by the poor within the church may indeed serve to focus attention on the unjust structures in society, but not at the expense of truth-telling, repentance, love, daring imagination and sensitivity within the church on the part of rich and poor.

I do not know if the denominations have the strength to look again at what the New Testament suggests about the relation between wealth, poverty and the proclamation of the gospel. I am certain, however, that if the denominations took seriously the interlaced callings of evangelism and the remedy of poverty, the nature of the life of the church on a local, national and international level would be transformed beyond recognition. The implied interchange of gifts and resources between congregations and individuals, and the implied presence of rich and poor one to another, would reflect the life of God. If such presence and exchange were to be seen in but one hamlet, village or city, our mouths would be open wide with wonder and the mouths of the cultured and not-so-cultured despisers of Christ would be closed.

2.

The link between the proclamation of the gospel and the remedy of poverty is, upon reflection, apparent, but more must be said if the point I have been trying to make is to have the force and effect it should. Something more specific must be said both about the view Christians ought to have of money and about the norms of behavior and virtuous habits this view implies.

Looking back over the history of the church, two lines of thought appear over and over again. One is that our money and possessions belong, like our lives, not to ourselves, but to God. What we have, we have as a trust. We are not owners but stewards, permitted to use the property of God to meet our needs. The property, which belongs to God, is to be used first of all for his purposes and for his glory. The second line of thought is based on the image of giver and receiver: God is a generous master or parent who bestows blessings. Among them are the necessities of life. These God's servants or children receive as gifts, and they are to be generous in return. The gifts God gives are to be shared—especially with those in need.

Both lines of thought converge to produce two norms that have, throughout Christian history, exerted enormous influence on the way Christians form their common life. The first is the practice of hospitality; the second is generosity. Both are virtues flowing from the belief that what we have belongs to God, or has been given by God, and so is to be used for God's purposes and for his glory. Accordingly hospitality and generosity are to be practiced not merely as a prudential exercise with those from whom we expect a return—family, friends or neighbors—but with those from whom we will not receive benefit—strangers, the poor, and most of all our enemies. It is in this context that generosity and hospitality mirror God's relation to us and so make God known.

There is, however, a third virtue and norm of equal importance, which does not flow in an obvious manner from the generating images of owner/steward, giver/receiver. I have in mind the virtue of simplicity. Its origin is twofold. In the New Testament money is thought to be an enormously powerful source of temptation. Jesus even personified it as a demonic power by calling it *mammon* (Mt. 6:24, Lk. 16:13). Jacques Ellul has pointed out how unusual this was.

> Here Jesus personifies money and regards it as a kind of God. Now, this by no means derived from contemporary usage. Jesus has not taken a denotation current amongst the people he was addressing, for it does not seem that a god of this name was known amongst the Jews and Galileans or amongst the neighboring Gentiles. . . . This personification of money appears to be a creation of Jesus himself, and, if such it is, it means that he reveals to us something exceptional, since Jesus does not customarily use these deifications and personifications.[37]

The exceptional thing Jesus reveals is the extraordinary power money has to lead us into temptation and so away from God. Money and possessions have a peculiar power to lure us into appropriating for ourselves and our own purposes things that belong to God. Money sparks an enormous temptation to base our lives on our own resources rather than upon God's generosity and mercy (Lk. 12:15–20). The attempt to possess what is not our own amounts, in the eyes of Jesus, to an attempt to do without God. According to the New Testament, this attempt at self-sufficiency produces an inability to follow Jesus and so become his disciple. It is harder for a rich man to enter the kingdom of heaven than it is for a camel to pass through the eye of a needle. Money's

terrible power stands in part behind the oft-repeated warning
that runs throughout the synoptic gospels, that those who
try to save their lives will lose them and those who lose their
lives for Christ will save them. Simplicity is a norm for Christian living because money and possessions can do much
harm to the spirit. Simplicity is also a virtue; if we have an
overabundance of goods, we have them, in all likelihood, at
another's expense. The Epistle of James in particular suggests
that there is no accumulation of riches that does not involve
some injustice (Js. 5:1–6). This perception appears again and
again among Christians and it always suggests that simplicity, like generosity and hospitality, is a mark of the Christian
life—one that leads more deeply into the life of God, gives
expression to God's love, and displays that love to those
who do not yet know it or believe it.

How are the norms and virtues of hospitality, generosity
and simplicity to find expression in the lives of individual
Christians and in the common life of the church? It is enormously important to note that the church has always been
more hesitant to lay down a rule of practice about money
than it has to lay down a rule about sexual relations. It is
doubtless true that the church has for quite pusillanimous
reasons failed time and again to raise with sufficient force
the issue of what we have and what we do with it, yet it
would be untrue to suggest this reluctance is due simply to
collusion with anxiety and greed. Reticence concerning this
matter stems from a recognition that the disposition of wealth
has more to do with the leading of the Holy Spirit and the
exercise of imagination than it does with detailed practices.

All Christians live in the tension between this age and
the age to come; all occupy a particular place in society; all
have their own history and their own obligations and needs.
For these reasons it is not right to lay down one practice of
hospitality, generosity and simplicity for all. The search for
the obedient way on the part of each Christian will involve
courage, patience and more than a little boldness. It will
involve faith, hope and love. Most of all, it will require prayer,

the presence of God's Spirit and, on our part, the use of all our art and creative imagination. Indeed, the great fault of the church in respect to money is not its reluctance to articulate rules, but its failure to call forth imagination in the service of love.

It seems that in all areas of life the living of the Christian life becomes, at a certain point, a matter of art and imagination. Nowhere is this more obvious than in the disposition of worldly goods. No matter what disciplines we may espouse, it is in the end art that must shape our use of money, but the art of using money is not free to take any shape. It rests upon a necessary presupposition—that what we have belongs to God rather than to ourselves—and it must find expression along certain well-defined lines. The lines God in his love always sketches are hospitality, generosity and simplicity. What God gives is the freedom to paint within these lines in a full spectrum of colors.

The remarks and observations I have made thus far seem to me to be the first ones Christians are called upon to make when they speak about wealth and poverty. A pressing question remains unanswered, however, and the liberation theologians are right to press it. What relation exists between evangelism on the one hand and political activity designed to remedy poverty on the other? Do Christians have *political* obligations to the poor? This is the question Gutierrez raises in his third point about the Biblical meaning of poverty. Poverty is not only material poverty and openness to God. It is also "a commitment of solidarity and protest." We have given attention to the first two meanings. Now is the time to focus on the third.

For Gutierrez and other liberation theologians, the first connection between evangelism and the remedy of poverty is political. To preach the gospel is to identify with the poor, and true identification involves throwing one's weight behind those political (and perhaps military) forces that favor the cause of the poor. Gutierrez' moral seriousness is apparent on every page, but what he says about mandatory identification with political causes and movements is more of an assertion than a necessary implication of exegesis. The self-emptying of God in Christ and the fact that Jesus spent much of his time with the poor in no way entails a particular political conclusion. Yet although Gutierrez draws conclusions that go beyond anything his exegesis warrants, he does stress the necessary question: Do Christians have *political* obligations to the poor? Is the activity such obligation implies, like the obligation to care for the church's poor, inextricably linked to the message the church is sent to proclaim?

By stressing the themes I have stressed, I do not mean to imply that the state of the poor is a matter properly addressed *only* through preaching and voluntary acts of love, or that the state of the poor presents believers with no moral questions concerning social institutions and movements. I do believe, however, that the argument I have made to this point raises questions about the priority now given by liberation theologians and many other Christians to political activity. Unless the biblical themes I have identified are given the emphasis they deserve, the *necessary* link between proclamation and the remedy of poverty will be severely weakened, or perhaps even cut. Then both evangelism and care for the poor will be collapsed into, or set in opposition to, political action.

When this happens, as at present it does, the evangelistic voice of the church is muted and its self-understanding distorted. The primary reason this occurs is that even though political activity is mandated by love, it masks love's face in a way that evangelism and direct care of the church's poor do not. Political judgments are so difficult to assess that, even if we could show that our political acts ought always to benefit the poor, we would be hard pressed to prove that the political course we advocate is the only one or the best one to follow. More important, the remedy political (or military) activity offers for the disease of poverty always involves the use of compulsion and the threat of force, carrying with it the seeds of another illness—an illness which, not always but often, has proven worse than the disease which preceded it. Every political gain has its cost. If we increase liberty, we always do so at the expense of some aspect of justice, and vice versa. Politics is always a game of relative gain and loss in which one group gets its way at the expense of another.

Evangelism and political activity may indeed spring from the same motive, but in this age, their inner connection is to non-believers (and often to believers) at best obscure and at worst nonexistent. What is much more striking and clear is that obligation linking all Christians, no matter what their political or economic views—to preach the gospel to the ends of the earth and, while there is yet time, to do good for all people, especially those of the household of faith.

In avoiding the mistaken notion that Christian belief can provide us with a political program, we must not fall into the equally mistaken view that Christian belief has nothing to do with our political and economic life. If the Christian left sometimes forgets that the message it proclaims and the politics it espouses are not identical, the Christian right also tends to forget that its message carries an implied criticism of all forms of social order and an invitation to change. Participation in the common life of the church can provide Christians with metaphors, images, skills and power to undertake with all people the common human task of creating a social order that furthers liberty, justice and welfare for all. The images that Christian belief provides to grasp and shape social life are the most adequate we have. In a post-Constantinian age, they can be used and defended by Christians in the public forum, even if Christians refrain from using the religious source of their social vision as a means of its justification. In the public forum, Christians will, like all people, have to provide good reasons for accepting their vision of society over some other vision.

I want to provide a single example of how the Christian view of monetary relations within the church can and ought to shape their view of monetary relations in society. I want to show as well that Christian belief does carry economic implications even if it cannot and ought not to dictate economic policy. The question is, does Christian belief carry with it a vision of society that provides both an invitation to economic reform and a standard for judging the moral quality of our economic order? Does life in the body of Christ suggest the way in which we ought to view the economic relations of society in general? Does this way of seeing (and living) exert pressure in the direction of reform and transformation, rather than in the direction of social withdrawal or unbending attempts to keep things as they are?

The answer to all of these questions is yes. Economic relations within the church ought to be governed, we have said, by certain basic notions and principles. The most important of these are:

1. Christians live as part of a body which is one, yet has many members;
2. each member of the body contributes to the common good of the whole through his or her particular gifts, and each benefits from the common good by receiving the gifts of others;
3. each member is then dependent upon and indebted to all the others; and
4. since each contributes to and benefits from the common good, no member ought to be prevented from making their particular contribution, nor should they be prevented from receiving benefit.

In the previous discussion all these points have been made, even if not in such an unvarnished manner. Do they have more general social implications? Do they suggest anything about the way in which Christians ought to view the economics of society as a whole? If we assume that life in the church is not utterly discontinuous from life in society as a whole, it is reasonable to assume that the images one uses to understand life in one sphere ought to be used to understand life in another, analogous, one. If the life of the church is rightly compared to that of a living body, then the life of society as a whole ought also, to the degree that there are similarities, be understood by means of the same image.

If this image is used as a window through which to view the present economic organization of American society, what is the pattern of light and shade that is apt to appear? The image forces upon us critical questions about an economic system like our own, one that prevents large numbers of people from making a contribution to the common good and also deprives them of its benefits. Structural unemployment that yields a pool of cheap labor cannot be a morally acceptable social goal. And it will not do to say, as have some critics of the Roman Catholic bishops' pastoral letter on the American economy, that economics is a matter of impersonal forces rather than of morals. To allow such a claim is to abandon the moral enterprise to fate, and surrender our ability to form the kind of society we want to live in.

The point I have just made may not at first appear to have bite, but it does. The image of a body with many members suggests both a goal for economic life and a standard of judgment. The image does not yield economic policies we are morally required to hold. Economic policy, like political policy, is a matter of art and intelligence. The image does, however, give us a direction in which to head and a fixed star from which we can take our bearings along the way. Furthermore it is an image that is capable of moving us to be critical when we are tempted, for selfish reasons, to be complacent, and one that has power to motivate us to action. In Victor Turner's words, the image of the body proves to be both a storehouse of meaning and a powerhouse capable of producing action.[38] Its analogical extension to the political economy thus invites both critical observation and attempts to reform or transform the economy in question. The images learned within the common life of the church can and ought to be extended to other forms of life. This extension provides a way to grasp the nature and purpose of these relations, a point of vantage to assess their moral quality, and the vision and motivation to seek their improvement.

None of these results follows automatically from Christian belief. Blindness and disobedience are ever-present human realities; Christianity, like all other beliefs, cannot guarantee political wisdom or moral sensitivity. It does, however, carry with it a very definite vision of the nature of human society, a vision that has remarkable power to move people to the task of social transformation. In respect to the shape of our economic system, the implications of this vision are quite extraordinary and unsettling. It provides at one and the same time a way to see the truth about our economic relations both within the church and within society as a whole, and it calls us out of ourselves to do or live the truth we see. The presence of such vision and power in human affairs is no small thing. Upon it the healthy common life depends.

POWER AND AUTHORITY

The time has come to raise the most crucial and difficult problem of social ethics—the problem of power. At the outset I want to do two things, and the first is to make some observations and proposals about the disposition and use of power both within the church and within society as a whole. The second is to clarify and defend the general thesis that, even though the first task of Christian social ethics is the constitution of the church, the metaphors and forms of life present within the Christian fellowship can provide a source of vision and strength for Christians to undertake with all people the common human task of creating, maintaining and reforming social order.

In conjunction with this second aim, I hope to render an even stronger thesis more understandable and more convincing. I want to argue that Christian belief and practice provides, by analogical extension, the most adequate basis for social life in general—even though the social vision and way of life Christian belief suggests must, in discussion of public policy, be recommended and defended by the provision of "good reasons" potentially acceptable to everyone, rather than by direct reference to religious belief and practice.

There is no more strategic means to explain and defend a position like the one I have just sketched than by a discussion of power. In its disposition and use we can see most clearly the relation between life in the church and life in society. Power provides the crucial test case for my argument, but discussion of power always warrants care and caution; power can do such enormous harm. Power is the ability of an individual or group to achieve their purposes, but everyone knows that human purpose can degenerate to the level of whim, or it can become evil. When power is yoked to whim, it becomes "raw" or "naked," and when it is linked to evil intent it becomes corrupt. In either case, we are right to tremble.

The discussion of power demands care and caution for another reason. Of all the human drives, the quest for power is both the strongest and the most hidden. Power is a subject seldom discussed without an enormous amount of heat and self-deception. Sexual drives, despite the many obscure byways they take, have a way of making themselves plainly felt and visible; cupidity has the same proclivity. But the drive for power hides itself behind countless masks, for it is the nature of power itself that so tempts us to cloak our drive to attain it. Power is the ability to attain purpose, but what happens if we do not know our purposes or will not admit to them? Then our quest will manifest itself in indirect and disguised ways; it will leak and ooze rather than find open and accountable expression.

To admit to our purposes is to take responsibility for them. To take responsibility is to grow up because, like grownups, we take upon ourselves both success and failure, good and evil. The drive for power is hidden because it is such a fearful thing to look directly upon what we are up to in this life.

Most people and groups prefer not to look, and so hide their drive for power from themselves and others. Thus when we make an inquiry about power, we stand face to face with the drive that tempts us most to deception. Care and caution, then, are the most minimal prerequisites for the investigation about to be undertaken. Honesty and courage are also required, as are the three great virtues of faith, hope and love. Apart from them we will do little more than add deception to deception.

Power is, first of all, simply a fact of life; it is never absent from human affairs. In itself it is neither good nor bad, and despite utopian dreams and schemes to the contrary, there will never be a community in which it is not present in one form or another.

The ethical question about power is not, therefore, whether we should or should not have it among us, but how we ought to order its possession and use. The traditional way of posing this question is to ask about the relation between power and authority. Generally speaking, we believe that power is rightly possessed and used if the people having it and using it have the *authority* to do so. If the theoretical and moral issues connected with authority are solved, those connected with power are solved at the same time.

Social ethics can address the issue of power only by discussing that of authority, and the best place to begin is simply to ask what authority is. It needs to be said no simple definition is possible, but there are observations to be made that are of enormous help.[39]

We can note first of all that there are currently two bases upon which authority is justified. One view is that the legitimacy of authority depends upon more basic social agreements. Members of a given society bestow authority on institutions or people that reflect, embody, or promote generally shared beliefs, values and intentions. Hannah Arendt has reminded us that this point of view requires two necessary assumptions if it is to be convincing. It assumes a common set of beliefs and values to which all or most members of society subscribe, and it assumes that there are certain people who stand closer to these beliefs and values than others and have skills others do not have to further them.[40]

The difficulty of making the first of these assumptions

has produced a second view, namely, that authority is based not upon the presence of shared beliefs, values and intentions, but upon their absence. People who are not unified in their beliefs and purposes must submit to common rules so that common life and action become possible. In this case authority does not further common belief and purpose, but compensates for its absence.

In speaking of authority, a distinction is often made between being "an authority" and being "in authority." "An authority" is to be followed or obeyed because of knowledge, judgment or personal qualities. Such a person is to be listened to or obeyed because of an ability to give an authoritative interpretation of a body of belief or knowledge or way of life regarded as binding or paradigmatic, and in so doing strengthen the foundations of social life. On the other hand, when we speak of those "in authority" we need not imply common values. We need imply only that they have the right by virtue of their position or office to make binding decisions. What matters about those "in authority" are not their beliefs or personal characteristics, but the social or institutional place they occupy.

A third observation about authority is the importance of distinguishing it from other means of social control, such as coercion and persuasion. People who have authority are often licensed to use coercive measures, but they must give some justification for the particular measures they take. Coercive power, pure and simple, gives no such account. It is this observation that forces us to distinguish authority from persuasion, for persuasion cannot use coercion and at the same time remain persuasion. Thus however we understand it, authority seems to be a means of social control that lies between coercion on the one hand and persuasion on the other. It must be prepared to use both, but it cannot be identified with either.

What conclusions do these observations suggest about the nature of authority? It might be possible to get everyone to agree that authority, as opposed to coercion or persuasion, is the right that some people have to expect others to listen to and follow their decisions, and to exert coercive pressure of one sort or another if they do not. This definition covers social, political and institutional authority, and is generally acceptable, but it leaves all the important questions unanswered. The basic questions about authority and the moral use of power are, first, whether authority is based on widely shared beliefs, values and intentions, or on their absence, and second, how being "an authority" is related to being "in authority."

I hope to show that, in the end, both these questions are moral ones. The real issue is not how things are, but how they ought to be. I want to argue both that authority *ought* to be rooted primarily in shared beliefs, values and intentions (and only secondarily in their absence) and that being "an authority" *ought* to be a moral precondition in society for being put "in authority." I should like also to establish that the common life of the church should make this position clear and convincing to Christians and that they in turn can recommend it with good reasons to society as a whole.

In classical times an *auctor*, or authority, was one who furthered the common beliefs and purposes of a people. As I have already suggested, in societies like those of Western Europe and North America it is now an open question as to whether there is any longer a common set of beliefs and purposes to further. Alasdair MacIntyre argues strongly that secularism and pluralism have removed any possibility of our having a sufficient number of shared beliefs to support this classical notion, and that our diversity is so extreme that we can no longer "solve" the moral and social issues confronting us. We are, he believes, in a disastrous situation.[41]

A number of other political philosophers and social analysts have reached similar conclusions, but have not thought their implications to be as foreboding. Richard Friedman looks at the same facts and concludes that we can get along quite well with a notion of authority based upon the absence of shared values and purposes, and that we need not have recourse to the notion of "an authority" save in the sense of an "expert." Making Friedman's point in even stronger terms, Bernard Mayo and Thomas Wren argue that it is a fundamental error to think of political authority in *personal* as opposed to *institutional* terms. People possess authority within organizations because of a system of offices, rules and directives. Authority depends, therefore, not upon personal characteristics but upon status, and upon the directives and rules of the institution. If anyone holds office and if their commands are not contrary to what is directed or permitted by the rules, they are to be obeyed. They need not to be "believed." Thus Mayo concludes, with considerable emphasis, that the authority of rules comes before the authority of persons. Being "in authority" is prior to being "an authority," and the use of the latter term in any sense other than "expert" ought to be jettisoned from our social and political vocabulary.[42]

This position has many other defenders; it catches well the spirit of the age. In the West we strive to maintain open and diverse societies with room for countless beliefs and goals. Freedom and diversity are the values we prize most highly. What we ask of authority, therefore, is not that it further our common beliefs, but that it provide a free and relatively just order within which we can hold our own beliefs and pursue our individual plans. Authority helps us to achieve our goals and ensures that as each person pursues their particular "life plan" they do not, through ignorance or selfishness, rob others of the same opportunity.

Reactions from both the left and the right to the atomism of our dominant cultural point of view will, I suspect, become stronger as the years progress. Against the individualism of the present age the reactions from both left and right will be collectivist in nature, for the problem of the one and the many does not disappear from political ethics any more than it does from theology and metaphysics, or from sexual and economic ethics. If the pendulum swings too far toward diversity, one can expect a countermovement toward unity and vice versa.

It follows that we should expect a number of attempts to show the inadequacy of the prevailing view of authority and to restate and defend the classical view that it ought at any rate to further common values, and that those "in authority" ought to *be* authorities in the sense already outlined.

Such a countermovement should amount to a frontal assault on the basic premises of classical liberalism, namely, that belief and value are private rather than social issues, and that authority *ought* only to be exercised to prevent one person from wrongly depriving another of liberty. The very writers who defend the liberal view of moral value and authority also admit that people "in authority" can and do disobey, misapply, neglect and wrongly construe the rules and directives they are supposed to administer and enforce. Whether these things are done out of wickedness or foolishness, they are nonetheless done. It is a disturbing fact that the most wonderful system of rules can be subverted by those "in authority." It is also the case that the greatest threat to free and democratic government is not corruption, but demagoguery. Corruption can be held in check by laws and sanctions, but demagoguery thrives on the very freedoms the liberal democracies allow.

Some abuses of authority are not infractions of the rules and cannot be effectively held in check by rules. Our social institutions are at this point dependent upon the moral relationship that exists between office holders and private citizens. Finally, it would appear that a moral community is necessary if our system of rules is to survive without subversion from their intended purposes. One recent commentator puts the matter in this way:

> Perhaps the notion that we are a society of laws and not men has come to be taken too literally. . . . The very nature of the law is such that it is incapable of being a sufficient conception of the public good. Law cannot be

coterminous with public authority; at best it can only represent the stable, durable core of such authority.[43]

"Law cannot be coterminous with public authority." Neither can bureaucratic rules, directives and policies; they all must be interpreted, applied and enforced by moral agents. For this reason alone it would be morally disastrous to discard the idea that a person "in authority" ought also to be "an authority"—and a protector and augmentor of a moral community. The Nixon White House tried, as have countless others, to accomplish just such a separation. The results are plain for all to see.

Another point at which the classical notion of authority seems morally necessary is in the pursuit of social goals. If we attach authority *only* to an office and the rules and directives that surround it, we make it impossible for those "in authority" to be in any way responsible for those goals and purposes. It was Adolf Eichmann's defense to say that he was only a functionary within a system. He argued that, as the executioner of millions of Jews, he acted not as "an authority" but only as one "in authority"; he only did what he was ordered to do. Responsible only to the rules and directives governing the institution in which he functioned, he had, he claimed, no moral responsibility for the goals pursued by that institution, even if it was the Third Reich.

So a view of authority based only on roles, rules and directives does not seem adequate. Some idea of a moral community to which both people and institutions are responsible is morally required, as well as the idea that those who hold office ought to share the beliefs and aspirations of the people they serve. They should possess special qualities and skills necessary to take responsibility not only for protecting but also for furthering these beliefs and purposes.

The points I have made in defense of the classical view of authority strike responsive cords in most people, but they also cause red lights to flash. Those influenced by classical liberalism will be troubled by the repressive connotations of phrases like "a moral community" or "an authority." They will want to place restraints both on our social institutions and upon those who hold office in them, but, at the same time, they do not want either our institutions or our authorities to enforce a body of belief and purpose they may not share. As a result, I think most people feel themselves to be on the horns of a dilemma. They feel the need for a moral community, but fear its repressive possibilities; they fear they will purchase unity at the price of their own liberty and distinctiveness.

Our current social notions suggest two ways to get off the horns on which we find ourselves tossed about. Both have wide appeal. Both have avid supporters. Both, in the end, only make matters worse.

The first suggestion is to get rid of the need for a moral community, and the authority that exists to protect it, by substituting the notion of common *interest* for that of the common *good*. Thus political societies do not exist to pursue good, but to pursue interest. The advantage of such a maneuver is not only that it apparently avoids the worrying possibility of government being used to protect and further moral notions all do not share, but also that it is realistic. In politics we pursue interests rather than good, and so public authority ought to serve the former rather than the latter. On the surface the move from good to interest has much to recommend it, but the problems that arise are in the end greater than those supposedly discarded. Not all our "interests" are as vital or as worthy as others; some are neither, but rather the expression of pride, greed and envy.

How can the public interest be discussed apart from a moral standard by which we can measure its moral quality? The attempt to substitute interest for moral good in the end fails even in the sphere of public affairs; "interest" turns out to be a moral as well as a descriptive category. Another reason this suggestion fails is that public interest, apart from some common moral standard, has an ineluctable tendency to become the interest of the stronger. Interest, even public interest, is always assessed from a point of view. One thing the Marxists have reminded us of again and again is that interest looks different depending on where one stands in the social order. Manufacturers of munitions and migrant farm workers will not see the public interest in the same way. Apart from a common set of moral norms, the public interest will certainly turn out to be the interest of the stronger, and it will be purchased at the expense of those who can least afford it. Apart from common moral norms, authority will further only the interests of some. Once again, the attempt to subordinate authority and so power to *interest* rather than to *good* raises a specter far more dread than the one it was to banish.

A second way to separate morality and authority is to say that social and political questions are all, in the end, factual. What is needed is objective, scientific research, from which we can derive public purposes and techniques of social management to judge both our institutions and those who hold authority in them. Alasdair MacIntyre has, in recent years, made an important observation about the sort of social roles that dominate when this "objective" point of view is in the ascendant.[44] A society that insists on viewing its common life in a purely factual manner tends to produce a certain cast of characters: the expert, the manager and the therapist. Crudely stated, the expert gathers and interprets the necessary factual data, the manager masters and applies the findings of the experts, and the therapist helps people make a satisfactory adjustment to the social world that the experts and managers create.

In a morally neutral society it is this cast of characters that supports those "in authority" and comes to occupy many of the most powerful positions. The expert, the manager and the therapist are seen as "authorities" not because they further common beliefs and values, but because they are masters of the facts. MacIntyre has done the public an enormous service by uncovering this most recent attempt to get along without a moral community, as well as by showing that the attempt must fail. The social sciences have not established sociological and psychological laws, and their findings are not objective and morally neutral. The expert, the manager and the therapist only mask their own values and purposes behind a facade of objectivity, using this facade as a screen behind which they pursue their own goals. Sometimes the attempts of those "in authority" to mask their own commitments and place them beyond question can become comic. Every new administration assembles its own battery of experts, conducts its own "in depth" studies, and comes up with "new findings" showing that the crowd now "in authority" were right all along. The growing mistrust of experts, managers and therapists, not to mention public officials, is more than merited; their "objectivity" is a ruse for the acquisition of power that frees its users from general scrutiny.

Despite the dangers involved, it would seem that society cannot remain healthy without a set of beliefs, values and purposes that provide unity and a common moral reference by means of which authority can be exercised and judged. The reduction of moral concerns to "interests," "facts," or "private ideals" opens the way for forms of injustice and authoritarianism we are right to fear. One would think that of all the groups in society who ought to see the danger involved in these attempts, the Christian denominations would be among the most prominent and the most vocal. Indeed the decline of moral standards in the conduct of business and public affairs has elicited cries of alarm that are sincere, but on the whole ineffective. For a host of reasons, the denominations seem unable to arrest this decline of public standards. Given my earlier premise, it is perhaps not surprising that the denominations prove increasingly ineffective as social forces. Their lack of power is even more understandable when one realizes that they have adopted the same view of authority as the society. Clerical and lay leadership is made up increasingly of experts, managers and therapists, social roles that provide generative models for those "in authority" in the denominations.

Thus the "ministry," both lay and clerical, becomes increasingly professional. Those "in authority" are largely those with technical skill and professional training that serves the interests of the denomination's clientele. From behind the cover of their particular expertise, they enlist the general support of their constituency for the particular causes and interests to which they are committed. These professionals are the ecclesiastical counterparts of the experts who fill the executive posts in our corporations and government agencies; what they are not, on the whole, are people with a deep knowledge of Christian belief and practice that is coupled with a tested wisdom.

In short, the denominations do not offer an alternative to the moral evisceration of political and social authority; they simply mirror it. Because they blend in so well with the environment, the denominations have forfeited any real chance they might have to make a prophetic witness or, better, to provide a prophetic alternative to the moral disarray. At times denominational aping of secular ways of obtaining and exercising authority borders on the ridiculous. In my own denomination, one that prides itself on having "the historic episcopate" as a means of guaranteeing continuity with the teaching of the apostles and with the polity of the early church, the members are now regularly treated to the sight of those who have succeeded as experts, managers or therapists "running" for the office of bishop. To be successful, a candidate must put together a "package" that will satisfy the "interests" of a sufficient number of groups to guarantee election. The question is, "How does candidate A stand on issue X?", which is not the sort of question that reveals whether or not a prospective office holder is in any sense "an authority."

Such a process of election is, within my own denomination at least, generally admitted to be both depressing and humiliating. Most everyone knows something is wrong; not many people know exactly what. In my denomination and in many others, the membership have lost a way of ordering power in the community that makes the necessary connection between being "in authority" and being "an authority." Is it any wonder that those "in authority" in the denominations are viewed with the same suspicion and sometimes cynicism as their secular counter-parts? The good news is that most people sense that something has gone badly wrong, that those in authority over us do not embody and further the beliefs, purposes and ways of life that we share and hold dear.

2.

The obvious question, then, is whether or not there is a way ahead, one that allows us to have those "in authority" be also "authorities" in the classical sense without the fear of totalitarianism and the sort of collectivism that sometimes accompanies it. In regard to power and authority, we now come to a question we have had to ask previously about sex and money. Is there a better way ahead than that offered by our environing culture or by the adaptation to that culture on the part of the major denominations?

Once again, the other point of view for which we search emerges from the pages of the Bible. In respect to power and authority, it is the apostle Paul who offers the most obvious place for us to begin our reflections.[45] The portrait of apostolic authority emerging from the pages of Paul's letters certainly depicts the apostle as what I have called "an authority," yet there is an interesting and instructive twist. Paul appears to be "an authority" who is not "in authority"; he has authority in the church, yet he holds no office. The case of Paul provides a marvelous opportunity to look at a situation that is

the reverse of our own. In doing so, we can learn something
about how the two sorts of authority we have identified
ought to be related.

If we look at the authority Paul had in the churches
under his care, two things become apparent. One is that in
all the most important respects, Paul counts himself as being
like all other Christians. The other is that, as an apostle who
has seen the risen Lord, has been given a special commission
to proclaim the gospel, and can claim to have the mind of
Christ, Paul has power and the authority to use it. With both
power and authority he preaches, founds his congregations,
instructs them and orders their common life. If we can make
the relation between his identification with all Christians and
his special abilities and responsibilities clear, the picture of
Paul as "an authority" or *auctor* will come into focus, as will
the strengths and weaknesses of the sort of authority he
exercised in the church.

Paul's biography is in all the most important respects
like that of any other Christian. He speaks of his life as being
"hid with God." Through faith in Christ's death and resurrection, Paul, like all Christians, has died to an old life and
risen to a new one that he describes as "in Christ." Accordingly, he says that it is no longer he that lives but Christ
who lives in him; everything he now says or does is said
and done "in the Lord." His life is identified with Christ's
life—not in the sense that he or anyone else becomes the
savior, but in the sense that the life of each and every Christian ought to reflect the life and work of Christ.

As an apostle Paul has a special missionary vocation to
preach the gospel, but he is in no way called to speak or act
in ways that are fundamentally different from the ways in
which all Christians are called upon to speak and act. For
this reason, Paul can call on the members of the churches
with which he is associated to "imitate" him (I Cor. 11:1).
He does not mean by this admonition that he is their redeemer, but that, as his life and witness reflect Christ, so
ought theirs to do so in similar ways. In particular, Paul

means that the life of every Christian ought, like his, to show forth the mystery of the cross. Accordingly, he insists that if anyone boasts, they ought, like himself, to boast only in the power given to those who are "in Christ." As with Christ on the cross, God's power works in the life of believers in weakness and suffering rather than in the strength of their own lives and personalities.

Paul says, in effect, that neither his life nor the life of any Christian is their own, nor is he in a fundamental way different from any other follower of Christ. Both the apostle and the community are "in Christ," both are subject to the gospel in respect to what they say and how they live their lives. As one commentator has put it, "Both the church and the apostle are to be subordinate to the manifestations of the one gospel. Hence, singularity and unity coalesce."[46] In terms now familiar to us, "in Christ" both apostle and church become one in a new way and yet in their unity maintain a diversity of gifts. The important thing to note, however, is that in this unity Paul, despite his authority, is subject to judgment on the basis of the gospel. If he judges the church, the church also judges him. In making their judgments, both must make appeal to the same standard.

Paul is anxious to assert his unity with all Christians, yet he lays claim to a special authority. He has, he believes, both the right and the responsibility to order the common life of the congregations under his care and sort out their disputes. He exercises authority over what they say and the way in which they live their common life, yet at the same time he does not exercise his authority through office or through forceful imposition. Rather, Paul tries to win others to his point of view, by pointing to the power at work in him and by appealing to them to test what he says and does against their common belief in Christ. Paul seeks voluntary compliance, though he could exercise a power that would simply overwhelm, perhaps even destroy, his opponents (I Cor. 4:19; 5:5).

Let us look more closely at the authority Paul claims and

exercises. Like all the apostles, Paul was "a plenipotentiary representative whose task it is to conduct business independently and responsibly for the one who has assigned him these powers for a particular service."[47] As an apostle, Paul's authority does not rest upon a human source, but upon the commission of Christ himself. Although he, like the other apostles, is one of the pillars of the church, the continuing exercise of apostolic authority must be judged by the common faith of the church. Everything the apostles say and do must reflect Christ. Thus the authority they exercise must be tested by the community on the basis of the belief and way of life it shares with them. Paul's authority is not an alien force; it is reciprocally related to the life of the community it serves to build up.

We are now in a position to understand why Paul exercised authority in the way he did—not by imposition, but by trying to win agreement. We can see it most clearly in his instructions to the Corinthian congregation in reply to the questions they asked him about sexual ethics, marriage and divorce (I Cor. 7). Where Paul believes Christ himself has provided a specific teaching, he simply repeats that teaching as binding for all believers. For example, he insists it is a teaching of the Lord that if two people are Christians they are not to divorce, but are to seek reconciliation. (vv. 10–11). Even though the teaching of Jesus did not cover all the questions put to Paul, he insisted that these other cases had to be looked at "in Christ" and in his spirit. In instances not covered by a dominical teaching, the apostle and the church were called upon to conform their life to that of the Lord.

To be specific, there was no teaching of Jesus that covered cases in which believers found themselves married to unbelievers. In addressing this issue, Paul makes it clear that he gives his own view and not a teaching of the Lord. (v. 12) He clearly believes he has both a right and a responsibility to give such instructions, yet his purpose is to win free acceptance of the will of Christ rather than to impose his own opinion. Accordingly, he tells the Corinthians that believers should remain with an unbelieving spouse unless the latter chooses to leave. By remaining, believers may bring their partners into relation with Christ, but if the unbelieving partner chooses to leave, the believing spouse is no longer bound. They are free both to divorce and to remarry since "in Christ" they are called to peace (vv. 12–16).

Paul both exercises authority and seeks to gain assent to his teaching. We can see this desired combination of authoritative command and free response most clearly in the concluding remarks of this section of Paul's letter, where he says to the Corinthians, "I think I have the Spirit of God" (v. 40). A better translation than this one from the RSV is, "I too have the Spirit of God." There is some irony in Paul's statement; clearly he is reminding the Corinthians of his own spiritual power. Yet even here Paul assumes that he and the Corinthians share the same spirit and, if they listen to that spirit, they will come to similar conclusions. If they do not, then they must show by the same spirit that he, Paul, does not have the mind of Christ. Thus he both judges and seeks to form the common life of the church, but at the same time allows the church room to make its own judgments by referring them to a standard both the apostle and the community share.

Paul is an almost pure example of the *auctor*. He has authority but he is not "in authority." He has the right and the responsibility to order the life of the church, but he occupies no office. Indeed, it appears that Paul deliberately sought to avoid the creation of office and hierarchy so that everyone would be subject clearly and directly to Christ. In his remarkable study of authority and spiritual power in the early church, Hans von Campenhausen writes,

> For the truly astounding feature of the situation we must . . . consider the fact that Paul, who both as one called to be an apostle of Christ and as a teacher of his churches, is a man of the very highest authority, nonetheless does

not develop this authority of his in the obvious and
straightforward way by building up a social relationship
of spiritual control and subordination.[48]

Paul exercises authority by constant appeal to a common
faith and way of life, not by appeal to office. For him the
church is built not around a hierarchy of office, but around
a variety of gifts which must be ordered by the spirit of Christ
as interpreted both by the apostle and the congregation.

Among the various ministries and gifts Paul mentions
are prophets, teachers, helpers, administrators, bishops, and
deacons. These titles refer to people who have gifts, and
they confer authority insofar as the gifts are used to make
Christ known and to build up the church. The titles do not,
however, refer to an organizational structure composed of
well-defined offices. For the church of Paul is almost a pure
community, based more on alliance than hierarchy. Authority is exercised through spirit-filled people who have the
power to interpret and further a shared tradition. We can
see by isolating the example of Paul the importance of people
who, in the classical sense, function as authorities. We are
left, however, with a question, namely, can a commonwealth
that knows authority but not office survive?

The experience of the early church was that it could not.
Paul's vision did not disappear with his death, but contrary
forces soon made themselves felt and pushed relentlessly in
a direction he plainly did not favor. Hierarchy, office and
structure were not long in appearing. Among the strongest
pressures that produced these developments were perse-
cution, the increasing numbers in the church, the flagging
zeal of second-generation Christians, apostasy, schism, he-
retical teaching, lax morals and, perhaps, a general tendency
on the part of most people to want and to create hierarchy.
In response to these and other pressures, the early church
began in a slow and piecemeal way to evolve a more structured organization. The first signs of this development are
to be found in Acts, I Peter and Revelation, which make

reference to "shepherds," "guardians" of the flock, and elders with special responsibility for the welfare of the church.

In these early sources we can detect what might be called a "hierarchical feeling,"[49] but the lineaments of office are still indistinct and the elders are still intimately related to the community they serve. Hierarchy is incipient, but there is no hint of authoritarianism, nor is there present a view that distinguishes office by placing it above the community in which it functions.

Movements in this latter direction were, however, not long in appearing. I Clement, a letter written some years after Paul's death, stresses the authority of the office of bishop and insists that those officers of the congregation who apparently had been removed in a sort of ecclesiastical *coup d'etat* be restored to office. In making his plea Clement argues that the offices of the church were created by the apostles to ensure continuing order, and his concern for order leads him to a very different view of the congregation than that held by Paul. He does not speak of a mutuality of gifts and ministries, but of a mutually dependent hierarchy. Clement's concern throughout is with peaceful order. The order he supports is one in which office and status play a central role, and where mutuality is less a matter of gifts and more a matter of rights and duties.

Thus in Clement's writing there appears an unmistakable formalization of office and a generally accepted order in which bishops and elders have charge of congregations. The order they maintain is, furthermore, one that is valuable in its own right, justified as a general human good and not as a specific means of furthering the gospel. A notion of office is emerging that is attached only by fragile threads to the gospel message it is presumably meant to serve.

The same direction of movement can be traced in other writings of the period. For Ignatius, Bishop of Antioch, who had to contend with false teaching rather than factionalism, the health of the church depends upon the spiritual presence of its bishop. Around him gather the priests and deacons, and in concert they promote both the holiness and the health of the congregation. It is primarily the bishop, however, who ensures the harmony, agreement and sympathetic union of the church. The congregation is joined to the bishop as the church is joined to Christ, and Christ to God.[50] Though all Christians have the spirit and so are bearers of holiness, it is still the bishop in union with Christ who maintains the holiness, health and unity of the church.

Once again we find ecclesiastical office in danger of splitting off and destroying a reciprocal relation between office and community. With Ignatius the danger centers around the notion of a particularly holy office upon which depends, in a disturbingly passive way, the holiness of all.

Another point in this development where we can see the growing tendency of office to distance itself from the community in which it functions is in the pastoral epistles— I & II Timothy and Titus. Once again, the danger confronting the church is false teaching; the answer of the pastoral epistles is to emphasize teaching authority. Church officers are to serve as examples to the congregation, to act as judges, to correct the wayward, to manage the practical affairs of the congregation. Above all, however, they are to preserve the apostolic teaching with which they have been entrusted. This task is no longer carried out, as in the Pauline church, through a spirit-filled authority who interprets a living tradition about the life, death and resurrection of Jesus. Responsibility for the apostolic witness has become the province of a professional class of clergy who hold established offices given them for precisely this purpose. Clerical office is a profession to which one can aspire, where natural endowment seems more important than empowerment by the Holy Spirit.

Von Campenhausen's summary of these developments cannot be improved upon:

> No longer is there any mention of the active cooperation or responsibility of the congregation. The most we find is the admonition that Timothy must always be respectful

when correcting the elderly, or that he honor those Christian widows who are active as deaconesses. There is no longer any effort to achieve a living mutuality in the relationship between the official and the community, such as was still being commended in I Peter.[51]

A church without "living mutuality" has come a long way from the sort of church assumed in I Corinthians 7. The sketch I have given of these developments is only a sketch; it is, moreover, a sketch that is not beyond dispute. Nevertheless there is considerable agreement about the primary lines I have traced, and these developments have power to point out the way for which we are searching. As we now find it difficult to preserve a common life with an idea of office that requires no moral or spiritual authority on the part of those who hold it, so the early church found it impossible to maintain a common life with a form of authority that had no idea of office and very little institutional structure. The evolution of office seems a practical necessity.

Review of the early history of the church, therefore, suggests two simple lessons in general social wisdom. The first is that a healthy and enduring society requires that a link be made between authority, in the classical sense, and office. The second is that the health of society depends also upon maintaining a living relation between authority, office and the community as a whole.

These lessons appear to border on banality. Another lesson suggests itself, however, at once more practical and less obvious. Of the two dangers that confronted the early church, surrender to charismatic anarchy or the absorption of all spiritual power and authority into office, the second is the greatest threat to the denominations of our own era. With their professionalized clergy and their bureaucratically structured organizations, the denominations inveigh against the anarchy of the sects but the sects are not their real enemies. Their real enemies are themselves. For the near and present danger is the deadly, soul-destroying concentration of institutional power in the hands of a professional clergy that relies on the authority of office, that does not show itself to be a vehicle for the interpretation and augmentation of the Christian gospel.

As von Campenhausen has reminded us, "Ecclesiastical thinking at all periods inclines in the direction of a one-sided preference for office."[52] We have traced this tendency from Paul's spirit-filled congregations to the "catholic church" built around the office of bishop as liturgical, spiritual or pedagogical center. In each case, the development toward "catholicism" threatened to separate office from both the community of the church and the service of the gospel. The real challenge before the denominations today is to think of authority, office and community in a living way—in and through the Spirit, and for the proclamation of the Christian message. It appears that the real issue is not whether authority in the church functions by ordering various gifts and ministries within an unstructured community, or whether it functions through office to preserve apostolic tradition and peaceful order. The real issue is whether authority, be it linked to call, gift or office, serves to make the power of Christ known and available both to those who believe and those who do not yet believe.

In his study of authority in the thought of St. Paul, John Howard Schutz defends the general theory that authority is an interpretation of power and that office is an interpretation of authority.[53] This conclusion seems to me perfectly correct. We must learn that authority in the church exists first to interpret and make available the power that comes to the church and to each Christian through Christ; it must yoke power to Christ's purposes in such a way that we make that purpose our own. Offices and structures may be necessary to carry out these purposes—generally speaking they have proved useful. But whether useful or not, within the church both authority and office stand under the judgment of Christ and so also of the community in which his spirit is present. The criterion is the gospel of Christ, and those in authority are called upon to interpret and further the gospel tradition in the freedom given by the Spirit, rather than to reproduce it mechanically, or preserve it as a static memorial from the past, or impose it from above as an alien truth.

3.

We can pause for a moment now and ask once more the question with which we began our investigation. If authority in the classical sense is necessary for the moral exercise of power, is there a way to join authority, office and society to make a common life possible and yet avoid authoritarianism? In the ordering of power, in other words, can authority and freedom coexist peacefully?

In principle, the answer to this question is yes. Our brief historical survey suggests that because authority in the classical sense presupposes a shared framework of belief and practice, it assumes also a common standard by which the commands of authority are to be judged. Authority is not, in principle, opposed to liberty; it is not coercion; it assumes the possibility of free assent to its commands. That assent is given because people can recognize in the commands of authority an attempt to further common beliefs and intentions. Authority is not authoritarian. It requires a common framework of belief and practice, but neither uniformity of thought and judgment, nor universal agreement that its commands are necessarily the best. Given what the philosopher Michael Polanyi has called a *fiduciary framework* more or less common to a society, the commands of authority, even if not viewed as most judicious, still need not be seen as alien or authoritarian.[54] As long as the commands of authority lie within what we might call a circle of permissibility allowed by common belief and intention, they can be freely accepted—even if disputed or criticized.

Authority in the classical sense is not inimicable to freedom and can be joined successfully to office. To maintain links between authority and liberty, and authority and office, is not only possible, but right and good. What is not possible is to have this kind of authority among people who do not form a society, but are merely drawn together by interests temporarily shared. Among such people *only* the authority of office is possible; to them, the commands of authority of any sort may at any time appear alien. Their judgment will depend upon where they think their interests at the moment lie. That is why the only authority they recognize, the authority of office, has such a tendency to become a coercive force furthering not common interest, but the interests of the stronger.

What are the implications for the church's moral task in what we have discovered about the relations that ought to exist between power, authority, office and community? Christians believe that the power to love, as defined in the two great commandments, constitutes human destiny. It is God's purpose to draw all people into this destiny and to that purpose he yokes his own power. It follows that the first moral and religious task of the church in respect to power is to be a community in which authority and office serve to make the power of God available to all, and in so doing help the entire community fulfill God's purpose.

The denominations face a spiritual and moral struggle of enormous proportions. If they are to constitute themselves as servants of the gospel (churches), rather than institutions meeting the needs of a clientele and servicing the private commitments and ambitions of a professional class of clergy (denominations), they must bring about a reversal in their self-understanding and communal life. I have already suggested what such a reversal might imply for the ordering of sexual and monetary relations; the implications for power and authority are even greater. First of all, the managers, experts and therapists who continue to fill the organizational structures of the denominations must add authority to the technical skill and the power of office they already possess. They will have to learn to interpret the power they represent through the Christian tradition and in the Spirit, a task requiring far more theological and spiritual acumen than is now generally exhibited.

A revolution will also have to occur in the way most lay people conceive of the church and take part in its life, as all baptized Christians come to see themselves as vehicles of and witnesses to the truth and power of God. Through responding to a particular calling within the congregation, they will have to learn to see themselves as a gift. From this perspective those considered authorities will appear not as the skilled providers of religious goods and services, but as fellow workers whose authority is necessary or useful for the fulfillment of a common task. The combination of authority and office that results will help the many become one, while remaining diverse in their gifts and callings. Authority and office will then be linked to the common life of the church in such a way that the whole church is helped to display the mystery of God's purpose to unite all things in his Son, so that all people come to love God with all their heart, soul, mind and strength, and their neighbor as themselves.

What I have said about power and authority can be summarized in a way that links it with the preceding discussions of sex and money. Authority ought to function in the church to bring about a unity of purpose and action among people with different gifts and callings, and yet it must do so in such a way that the diversity of these gifts and callings is preserved and strengthened, rather than weakened or eliminated. It is a necessary means in the life of any community for preserving a healthy tension between the one and the many. What Christians know and experience "in Christ" is that love is the key to unity and diversity, both in the life of God and in the life of *adam*. Authority within the church is to order the loving power God gives his people, thus making it available to the church and to all its members.

We are now in a position to address, if only briefly, the question with which this chapter began. Can we extend by analogy the understanding of power and authority gained by participation in the life of a church to the life of society as a whole? Can this political and social vision be defended outside of any reference to its religious source? I believe that it can. Even though it would take a work of far greater proportions than this small essay to defend my thesis, we can, in closing, note the major points around which such a defense would turn.

There is a fundamental analogy from which others follow. Although society has a contractual element that is right and good, nonetheless it ought, like the church, to be understood first of all as a "body" with many parts, rather than as a collection of individuals bound together by contractual obligations. If the body politic is to remain healthy, furthermore, it ought, like the body of Christ, to be one in which power, authority, office and community are kept in dynamic harmony. None of these elements ought to split off from the others; together they should work toward a common good while preserving and encouraging the particular contribution of each individual member. Power, authority and office ought in both church and society to serve to unite the one and the many, uniting people in a common purpose while preserving and encouraging the liberty and unique characteristics of each.

The social vision that grows out of this analogy will, I think, carry with it three social commitments. First it will lead to an insistence that anyone who is placed "in authority" be also "an authority," for unless this connection is maintained, the institutions of society will be subverted from public to private purposes. The virtues and vices of those "in authority" are not irrelevant to the functioning of public office, and this knowledge will lead Christians to press a traditional question of political ethics—one that has not been asked much of late. They will ask not only what authority ought or ought not to do, but who ought and who ought not to be placed in authority. They will seek a public debate over a question modern political theory has tried to push aside: what qualities make a good ruler? Christians will insist that there are qualities which suit people for office, that those qualities define character, and that it is matter of public concern to agree on what those qualities are.

The second commitment implied by the analogy I have suggested is a dedication to expanding the shared purposes of society to include both common interest and common good. A Christian social and political vision will consider it morally questionable, and even harmful, to limit the common purposes of society to the sphere of interest alone. Societies do pursue interest, but they also pursue good—unless they do, they can be called societies only in the most minimal sense. It is true that public authority ought not to coerce people to seek what is good, but such authority can be used to create circumstances favorable to the definition and pursuit of a common good.

Third, a social and political vision of this kind will maintain what I have called a "fiduciary framework," or a universe of moral discourse. This universe must be sufficiently shared to make social life possible, and of sufficient depth to make it rewarding; the alternative is a plethora of subcultures and private worlds. People nourished by a vision of the body of Christ will consider it a public duty—perhaps their most basic public duty—to maintain and strengthen a framework of moral discourse of sufficient breadth and depth to make social life possible and rewarding.

Life in the church, the body of Christ, can teach this important lesson about life in the body politic. Both authority and power are yoked to purposes of more than practical significance, for they comprise what we hold to be the good life and, as a result, they must be stated and defended. A shared moral discourse is necessary if we are to do either, and if public purpose is to be brought under moral scrutiny. Otherwise public life degenerates, and public authority becomes either ineffective or authoritarian.

Power and authority in the church have to be subject to a higher good and purpose than the particular interests of those who hold office, or of those who put them there. People formed in a community that is meant to include all people, and which carries such a truth as part of its definition, will sense that what is true for the body of Christ should hold true by analogy for the body politic. They will sense that our chief public duty is the maintenance of a moral discourse that makes it possible to speak of a common good, so that our public and private purposes can be stated in moral as well as practical terms. They will sense, in short, that in both church and society the social exchange involved in the exercise of power and authority depends finally upon another more basic form of exchange—the communication of meaning through the speaking of truth. In the public arena they will be committed to speaking the truth about our common good as they see it, and prepared to defend their views with reasons all people can understand.

THE AUTHORITY OF TRUTH

In the preceding chapters I have attempted to give some idea of the context, foundations, task and subject matter of Christian social ethics, and the direction in which I believe Christian social ethics ought to be heading is clear. There remains still one aspect of social ethics that I have mentioned but not addressed directly, and it has to do with our most basic form of social exchange—the communication of meaning. Yet the communication of meaning has appeared as a crucial factor in all the areas of social exchange we have discussed; sexual, monetary and political exchanges all take place within a universe of meaning. Social life is never simply a matter of practical necessity. It is redolent with meaning. This observation holds whether the society in question is the church or the body politic.

We have seen that within the church all forms of social exchange ought to reflect God's purpose for human life. All should be united in God through his Son and yet, in that unity, retain their distinctive characteristics and gifts. Within the fellowship of the church, all forms of social exchange are meant to sustain their meaning and further this purpose. So, the chief ethical task before the denominations and our society as a whole is maintaining a universe of discourse that gives meaning and shape to our lives. To say this is to imply first of all that telling the truth becomes one of the primary duties of love, and that truthfulness is a necessary virtue if we are to be able to love. It is also to imply that the denominations must seek to become communities where truth is spoken and where truthfulness is nurtured.

Why are truth telling and truthfulness fundamental to the life of the church? If they are to mirror God's life and love, all forms of social exchange depend upon them. Think for a moment of each form of exchange we have mentioned, and the central importance of telling the truth will immediately become apparent. The one-flesh union of *the man* and *the woman* depend upon truthfulness as the only means of avoiding the lies and deceit that threaten their union. Only where there is truthfulness and truth telling can the two become one in such a way that they are naked, but not ashamed. Only where there is the ability to tell the truth can the two be open one to another, and so in fact become one flesh.

Think also of monetary exchanges within the church. How can rich and poor become one body, one family or one people in and through their exchanges, unless each tells the truth? There is a terrible truth the poor have to tell the rich, a truth that exposes the blindness, greed and arrogance that so often surrounds wealth. There is also a fearful truth that on occasion must be spoken to the poor, concerning the envy and rage that so often accompany privation and want. If this word is not spoken, then something other than the love of God will prevail.

Finally, think of the relations that ought to exist within the church between those who have authority and office, and the community as a whole. If those in office are to serve Christ, they must make their purposes clear and these purposes must be judged by the church. The right functioning of authority and office depend upon truth telling and truthfulness on all sides. Apart from such a dedication to truth, the purpose of both leadership and community will not be tested, purposes that are genuinely shared become impossible, and the center of community life will not hold.

To speak the truth with love and power also entails a struggle to *do* the truth. The church is far from a perfect society of love, and it never does more than struggle to be obedient to the vision of God that informs it. Yet that struggle is all-important if the truth about God and human history is to be seen and believed. Those who speak the truth about God must struggle to live it and so demonstrate its power. The truth of the Christian gospel is revealed by its power to transform our social relations; if that power cannot be seen, words remain powerless. Speaking the truth in love requires a struggle to do the truth in love; both depend in turn on knowing and recognizing the truth.

The church has always believed that God has given the key to understanding both his life and our own in the long history of his relation with Israel that reached its culmination in the life, death, and resurrection of Jesus of Nazareth.

The church believes that if we remember this story in all its fullness, the spirit of God will lead us into the truth of Jesus' life and ours. So it is a task of both religious and moral significance for the church to remember this story and to use it, rather than some other, to interpret divine and human life. Yet it is precisely the task of remembering and interpreting their foundational story that the denominations are most loath to undertake. Their aim is not to form common belief and practice, but to serve individual interest. Furthermore, what Bellah's 'mystic' types that now make up the major proportion of the denominational membership want is not a canonical story that creates both doctrine and a common way of life, but a more private account of meaning that better suits their own religious and moral tastes. Accordingly, the denominations will be tempted to encourage an indifference to both story and doctrine coupled with a supposed tolerance for diverse opinion. Indifference of this sort leads inevitably to the inability to perceive the truth about our relations with God and with one another. When that happens, Christian social ethics will be informed by some other story.

What I have said about many of the interpretations of sex, money and power now popular within the denominations indicates that these alternative stories and interpretations already have a firm hold and will not be easy to dislodge. To remember and rightly interpret a story that gives human life its meaning and shape is no easy task, requiring faith, hope and love along with the more modest virtues of courage and truthfulness. It requires the kind of bold speech found in Paul's letters, but not apparent in the theological indifference that now characterizes both the denominations and the experts, managers and therapists that comprise the ranks of their professional clergy.

Truth has authority. If the truth is both spoken and lived, it has a way of recommending itself and making its own way. Were the denominations to undertake the task of remembering their foundational story, and of trying once more to constitute a community of belief and practice based upon that story, the truth would have power to recommend itself even in a secular age like our own. Accordingly, the ordering of sex, money, power and language within the church would make an impact upon society as a whole, even if most of the members of that society were not Christian. When the truth is seen, when it is both spoken and lived, it has its own authority.

Although in a secular and diverse society it is neither possible nor right for religious belief to be a justification for public policy, such belief can still make a powerful impression on the public mind and public policy. Thus the example of the community's common life may make it easier to argue that the life of society should more closely approximate the common life of the church. A very concrete example comes to mind. Former students in the southern Sudan tell me that large numbers of Muslims have been attracted to Christianity because of the more humane way Christian husbands treat their wives. These changed patterns of relationship have had some effect upon the treatment of women in general, making it possible to propose and defend alterations in law and social practice more favorable to women. These alterations must be stated and defended in moral terms acceptable to all, but this defense is possible and credible because of the transformation of sexual relationships within the fellowship of the church. If the denominations are serious about speaking to public issues, they cannot do so convincingly unless their own common life provides an example that recommends itself to all.

Truth, both spoken and done, has a power of its own to move the imagination and the heart. I have been struck on numerous occasions by the frequency with which the Bible speaks of telling the truth as an obligation and mark of a community faithful to God. One reason for its importance is that its presence bespeaks genuine love, and so both expresses and makes possible the transformation of social relations in such a way that we become "imitators of God" (Eph. 5:1). Another reason is that speaking and doing the truth serve to expose wickedness. It is a necessary weapon in the battle with what the Bible calls the "principalities and powers," the powers of darkness. A struggle to live life "in Christ" serves to expose evil and overcome it, exposing the lies on which we so frequently base our relationships. The Bible speaks of the truth as "light," and the metaphor is apt. As light exposes darkness, so truth exposes falsehood. To do and speak the truth is to transform our exchanges of sex, money, and power so that they may display the mystery of God's life and purpose, and so serve to draw all people more deeply into that mystery.

NOTES

1. W.H. Auden, "For the Time Being," in *Collected Longer Poems* (New York: Random House, 1969), p. 136.

2. Søren Kierkegaard, *Either/Or*, vol. 2 (Princeton: Princeton University Press, 1971), p. 19.

3. Robert Bellah, "Discerning Old and New Imperatives in Education" in *Theological Education* (Autumn 1982): 23.

4. For Levi-Strauss' most succinct statement of this position, see his essay "Social Structure" in *Structural Anthropology* (New York: Basic Books, 1963).

5. Marcel Mauss, *The Gift: Forms and Functions of Exchange in Archaic Societies* (New York: W.W. Norton & Co., 1967).

6. See Emil Durkheim and Marcel Mauss, *Primitive Classification* (Chicago: The University of Chicago Press, 1967). The introductory essay by Rodney Needham makes precisely this point.

7. W.H. Auden, "For the Time Being," p. 183. For this discussion of the doctrine of the Trinity I am indebted both to Auden and to Arthur C. McGill's *Suffering* (Philadelphia: The Westminister Press, 1982).

8. Malcolm Macourt, "Toward a Theology of Gay Liberation" in Mal-

colm Macourt, ed., *Theology of Gay Liberation* (London: SCM Press, 1977), p. 25.

9. Una Kroll, *Sexual Counseling* (London: S.P.C.K., 1983), p. 33.

10. Paul Tillich, *Morality and Beyond* (New York: Harper & Row, 1963), p. 80.

11. James Nelson, *Embodiment* (New York: Pilgrim Press, 1978), p. 127.

12. Nelson, p. 143.

13. Nelson, p. 144.

14. Robert Solomon, "Sexual Paradigms" in *Philosophy of Sex*, ed. Alan Soble (Totowa, NJ: Rowman and Littlefield, 1980), p. 91.

15. Nelson, pp. 17–18.

16. Nelson, pp. 17, 21, 26, 29–30.

17. Solomon, p. 123.

18. Solomon, p. 96.

19. Solomon, p. 101.

20. Gerhard von Rad, *Old Testament Theology*, vol. 1 (New York: Harper & Row, 1962), pp. 146–47.

21. Karl Barth, *Church Dogmatics* III/4 (Edinburgh: T. & T. Clark, 1961), p. 117.

22. Verhard Eller, *The Language of Canaan and the Grammer of Feminism* (Grand Rapids, MI: William B. Eerdmans, 1982), p. 12.

23. Eller, pp. 14–15.

24. William Safire, "Principle versus Value," *New York Times Magazine* (August 12, 1984): 8.

25. See Alasdair MacIntyre, *After Virtue* (South Bend, IN: University of Notre Dame Press, 1981) for the most eloquent lament to date over the eclipse of the notion of virtue in our discussion of the moral life.

26. "America's Activist Bishops," *New York Times Magazine* (August 12, 1984): 14.

27. See Gustavo Gutierrez, *A Theology of Liberation* (New York: Orbis Books, 1973), pp. 258–275.

28. Gutierrez, p. 266.

29. Gutierrez, p. 295. For his discussion of the meaning of poverty, see pp. 287–302.

30. Gutierrez, p. 296.

31. For a useful presentation of a similar point, see Raymond Brown, *The Birth of the Messiah* (New York: Doubleday, 1977), pp. 350–355.

32. See Gutierrez, pp. 297–98.

33. I owe this rather nice way of putting the issue to my teacher Paul Ramsey. See his provocative study of our attempt to take charge of our environment through genetic engineering in *Fabricated Man* (New Haven: Yale University Press, 1970), p. 138.

34. Gutierrez, p. 297.

35. See Philip Turner, *New Directions in Ministry* (Cincinnati, OH: Forward Movement Publications, 1983).

36. Walter E. Pilgrim, *Good News to the Poor* (Minneapolis, MN: Augsburg Publishing House, 1981), p. 151.

37. Quoted by R. Mehl in "Money," *The Vocabulary of the Bible*, ed. J.J. von Allmen (London: Lutterworth Press, 1958).

38. For a summary of Victor Turner's discussion of symbols as storehouses of meaning and powerhouses of feeling, see Philip Turner, "Come Let Us Eat and Drink," *Anglican Theological Review* (November 1976): 113–123.

39. For the primary source of what follows see Richard Friedman, "On the Concept of Political Authority" in *Concepts of Political Philosophy*, Richard Flatham, ed. (New York: Macmillan, 1973), pp. 121–145.

40. See Hannah Arendt, "What Was Authority?" in Carl Friedrich, ed.,

Authority: Nomos I (Cambridge, MA: Harvard University Press, 1958), pp. 81–112.

41. For MacIntyre's presentation of moral diversity and the collapse of authority see Alasdair MacIntyre, *Secularization and Moral Change* (London: Oxford University Press, 1967); *After Virtue* (South Bend, IN: University of Notre Dame Press, 1981) and Alasdair MacIntyre and Paul Ricoeur, *The Religious Significance of Atheism* (New York: Columbia University Press, 1969).

42. Richard Friedman, "On the Concept of Political Authority," pp. 145–6. See also Bernard Mayo, *Ethics and the Moral Life* (London: Macmillan, 1958), pp. 12–64, and Thomas Wren, *Agency and Urgency* (New York: Precedent Publishing, 1974), pp. 125–128; Mayo, p. 162.

43. William J. Meyer, "Political Ethics and Political Authority," *Ethics* 86 (January 1975): 61–69.

44. *After Virtue*, pp. 60–102.

45. The following discussion owes much to the treatment of power and authority by John Howard Schutz in *Paul and the Anatomy of Apostolic Authority* (Cambridge: The University Press, 1975).

46. Schutz, p. 250.

47. Hans von Campenhausen, *Ecclesiastical Authority and Spiritual Power*, trans. J.A. Baker (Stanford, CA: Stanford University Press, 1969), p. 22.

48. von Campenhausen, p. 46.

49. von Campenhausen, p. 83.

50. von Campenhausen, p. 100.

51. von Campenhausen, p. 114.

52. von Campenhausen, p. 295.

53. Schutz, pp. 249–280.

54. For Polanyi's notion of a "fiduciary framework" see Michael Polanyi, *Personal Knowledge* (Chicago: University of Chicago Press, 1958), p.

267. For a use of Polanyi's ideas to which my own essay owes much, see Leslie Newbigin, *The Other Side of 1984* (Geneva: The World Council of Churches, 1983), pp. 17–27.

Cowley Publications is a work of the Society of St. John the Evangelist, a religious community for men in the Episcopal Church. The books we publish are a significant part of our ministry, together with the work of preaching, spiritual direction, and hospitality. Our aim is to provide books that will enrich their readers' religious experience and challenge it with fresh approaches to religious concerns.